My Time in Another World:

Experiences as a Foreign Correspondent in China

by Noël-Marie Fletcher

芳 妮

My Time in Another World: Experiences as a Foreign Correspondent in China
Noël-Marie Fletcher

Fletcher & Co. Publishers
© September 2018, Fletcher & Co. Publishers LLC.

Author & Photographer: Noël-Marie Fletcher
Interior design: Noël-Marie Fletcher
Cover design: Zita Steele
Cover photo: by Noël-Marie Fletcher

All rights reserved, including the right to reproduce this book, or portions thereof, in any form without written permission except for the use of brief quotations embodied in critical articles and reviews.

Cataloging-in-Publication data for this book is available from the Library of Congress.

Library of Congress Control Number: 2018907249.

Cataloging information
ISBN-10 1-941184-23-5
ISBN-13 978-1-941184-23-3

Second Edition
Published in the United States of America

Fletcher & Co. Publishers
www.fletcherpublishers.com

"This book takes a fresh and raw look at contemporary China, founded on a lived experience and totally free of prejudice, which is rare among Westerners."

— Guy Mettan, Executive Director of the Geneva Press Club

"An enjoyable memoir of a young American business reporter's venture into China during a time, the 1980s, when few Americans had yet visited the country. It's all here: the often-harrowing travel, the food and cultural challenges, especially from a woman's point of view. Even better for an armchair adventurer are endless encounters with the Chinese people, all with their own interesting stories and perceptions about Americans. I especially enjoyed the writer's personal memoirs and anecdotes mixing with an unfolding adventure that leads suddenly to a riveting eyewitness account of the buildup and aftermath of the 1989 Tiananmen Square Massacre. I was Noël-Marie Fletcher's editor in Southern California when she announced one day that she was moving to Hong Kong. This is what happened afterward: an enthralling, revealing journey through everyday China as it grappled during the 1980s to come onto the world stage."

— Jim Wasserman, Retired Associated Press, Sacramento Bee writer

Contents

Foreword | 6

Part 1: Hong Kong Prelude | 8

Chapter 1:
Journalist in Asia | 9

Part 2: Travels into China as
a Foreign Correspondent | 16

Chapter 2:
The First 30 Days | 17

Chapter 3:
Shanghai | 52

Chapter 4:
The Cultural Revolution | 80

Chapter 5:
Doing Business in China | 86

Part 3: China Correspondent | 130

Chapter 6:
Beijing Life | 131

Chapter 7:
Paloma | 160

Chapter 8:
Journalist Community | 167

Chapter 9:
Tiananmen Square | 182

Part 4: Final Months in China | 204

Chapter 10:
Post-Tiananmen Crackdown | 205

About the Author | 217

Books by Noël-Marie Fletcher | 218

Foreword

I grew up listening to the following stories from my mother, whom I credit with first introducing global influences into my life from my earliest years and encouraging me to have curiosity and respect for the world around me.

My mother's stories of her adventures in foreign countries and encounters with diverse people always fascinated me—not only because these stories were different and exciting, but because my mother always taught me something important or useful that she learned from her experiences. Using her adventures as examples, she taught me so much. About life. About inventions, customs and different approaches to everyday challenges. And also about something she valued most of all—profound and unconventional wisdom shared with her by people from foreign lands.

I also credit my mother with teaching me to be open-minded from an early age. Given the extremely challenging and at times frightening conditions my mother lived through in Beijing, it would have been perfectly natural for her to develop negative or prejudiced attitudes against China or its people.

My mother is extraordinary because she has no such prejudices. Although she told me from my childhood of hardships she experienced while living in Beijing, she expressed no sentiments of regret or resentment, nor did she assign collective blame to any people or political groups. Sometimes her journalistic travels in other regions were not always so much fun, either—sometimes there were misunderstandings, arguments or strange setbacks that arose from being a foreigner in a different country. My mother described these encounters to me, too. Yet not once did she ever speak ill of any group of people.

Instead, my mother has always impressed me because she has not only a deep respect, but sincere admiration for Chinese people, their history and culture. My mother's love of China and her high regard for Asian civilizations shaped my perspectives as youth and have had a transformative and positive influence on my life.

When I was a small child, my mother taught me how to speak words in Chinese and how to show respect to Chinese people in different ways. She taught me about the healthiness and intrinsic value of Chinese cooking. She collected many books written by ancient and contemporary Chinese poets, historians and intellectuals, which I read growing up. She demonstrated to me the beauty of Chinese art, thought and culture in so many innumerable ways. My mother's enthusiasm for China's rich culture is the reason why I can only think of Chinese cuisine when I think of home cooking and why, at age seven, I had already mastered the art of eating with chopsticks. It is the reason why I feel familiarity whenever I hear someone speaking Chinese with a strong Beijing accent, why I have collected Chinese music over the years, and why I feel at home in Asian environments.

My daughter Zita Ballinger Fletcher and I pose while having fun in Europe in 2017. Photo by Noël-Marie Fletcher.

My mother's strong example also motivated me as a professional. I eagerly studied foreign languages from an early age. As a youngster in school, I always told my classmates about my mother's adventures in China and how I wanted to become a world-traveling journalist someday when I grew up. This dream came true for me. Inspired by my mother's career choices, I successfully became a journalist, foreign correspondent and international traveler.

The stories you will find in this book are those I cherish as life lessons. I am glad that they are finally being published in a book and shared with the rest of the world.

— Zita Ballinger Fletcher

Part 1:
Hong Kong
Prelude

My passport photo in Hong Kong.

Chapter 1: Journalist in Asia

Believe it or not, living in Hong Kong as a foreign journalist at the doorway to mainland China was by no means a given that you would venture over the border into the mother country. Many journalists I knew at the Foreign Correspondents' Club in Hong Kong during the swan song of its colonial heyday displayed a perfect horror at the notion of even going into China. It was viewed as primitive, unfriendly, oppressive, uninteresting, and lacking in the exotic sensual savories offered in Bali and Thailand. The crowd around the bar mostly consisted of U.K. journalist expats with a smattering of Americans, Australians, New Zealanders, Canadians and South Africans. There were few women at the FCC—most of the women who were there worked in "softer" public relations roles or on magazines. I was among an even smaller group of women journalists who directly competed with men in the news business. At that time, the Chinese people at the FCC mostly worked behind the bar in servile roles, except for an occasional floozy or two in a darkened corner of the room giggling while entwined with a notable octogenarian foreign journalist with wandering hands.

Street scene in Hong Kong. Photo by Noël-Marie Fletcher.

Once I brought a Hong Kong Chinese journalist friend of mine from the South China Morning Post into the FCC for a drink and a meal. She was hesitant to accompany me due to fears of discrimination, but I persisted. I thought, "Who cares?" But it was a disaster. The presence of my guest was met with cool stares and reserved tolerance that lasted for the duration of our uncomfortable social outing. I never invited her there again as it was apparent she was unwelcome. I had broken an unspoken rule, which I didn't mind doing. However, I valued my friendship with my colleague, who worked alongside me and competed against me and my newspaper, the HongKong Standard. We had both been Supreme Court reporters and worked next to each other in the pressroom at the courthouse. I didn't want to subject her to that kind of mistreatment in the FCC again. At that time, the word for Hong Kong Chinese people was "locals" and "locals" were looked down upon, even though they vastly outnumbered the expatriates. Today, if you look at the membership of the FCC, you'll see a large presence of Chinese journalists among its members. But this was not the case in Hong Kong when I witnessed its final years as a British colony.

By the time my first trip to the mainland loomed several months after I'd arrived in Hong Kong from Palm Springs, California, I'd heard so many detrimental remarks about China that I was worried about going on a reporting trip there. I didn't speak Mandarin and hardly did any of my journalist friends at the FCC. Instead, they had acquired some useful taxicab Cantonese phrases despite living in Hong Kong for years. I once met an American business manager in Beijing who managed a joint venture there. When I asked him about his knowledge of the Chinese language, he replied: "I don't want to speak like them because I don't want to think like them." This sentiment was alive and well among many expat journalists.

I remember the first time I said a phrase in Chinese. It was while seated in an office in a swank modern building in the Central District of Hong Kong. My instructor was a sour-faced, heavy-set Chinese man paid to provide foreign journalists with rudimentary language lessons before they moved to the mainland. Like a parrot, I mimicked a phrase he carefully uttered and then I burst out laughing. It seemed incredible to me that I had just spoken in Mandarin Chinese. Never in my life would I have envisioned myself doing that or preparing to move to Beijing. I already spoke French and Spanish, but had never thought of learning an Asian language. Unable to read

A chauffeur arranges a British diplomatic flag on the car of the Governor of Hong Kong in 1986. A red carpet for an event is visible on the right. Photo by Noël-Marie Fletcher.

my mind or to understand the humorous disbelief with which I viewed my present situation, the instructor became rather nasty and snappish for the remainder of the hour as well as during the next few sessions. I quit the lessons, figuring I'd find another way to learn to speak Mandarin. I'm sure the instructor misunderstood my reaction to speaking those first few words in Chinese, but I didn't wish to share my private musings, especially with such a grumpy, humorless individual.

My first trip to the mainland came after I had been traveling extensively in Asia on reporting assignments for *The Journal of Commerce* newspaper, located at that time on Wall Street in New York City. This financial newspaper occupied an illustrious place in the history of American journalism. It was first published in 1827 and had been threatened with closure by President Abraham Lincoln. It was the nation's oldest daily business newspaper, specializing in international trade, shipping, energy, and transportation. Back then, it was part of the Knight-Ridder Newspaper Business Information Service, and my news competitors were reporters at *The Wall Street Journal* and Reuters wire service. I was always on good terms with my British colleagues at Reuters, but the Americans at *The Wall Street Journal* always remained aloof.

My American editor at the JOC was Phil Bangsberg (whose byline was P.T. Bangsberg). He wanted me to be in China for a month on assignment. I was to travel by myself. The first part of the journey would be by train to the Special Economic

A high-rise view of busy Victoria Harbour in the Central District of Hong Kong where I lived and worked, as did many foreigners on Hong Kong Island. Photo by Noël-Marie Fletcher.

Zone in Shenzhen. Then I would take a hydrofoil across the South China Sea to Guangzhou (Canton), next came an airplane trip to Nanjing (Nanking), travel by rail again to Hangzhou (Hangchow) and then I had to catch another long train ride to Shanghai before flying back home to Hong Kong. My itinerary was packed with interviews lined up through Chinese government ministries. I was to be meeting with a myriad of Chinese companies seeking overseas business deals and foreign joint-venture investments. It was during the heady days of China's modern Open-Door Economic Policy when the Chinese, under the post-1949 Communist regime, were relatively new to foreign trade. American companies drooled over potential sales to those 1 billion unseen mainland consumers, while Chinese enterprises eyed selling their wares. They also offered cheap labor to foreign businesses.

My experiences in China evolved from that first long trip to other journalistic jaunts to the mainland. A year or so later, I was posted by the JOC to Beijing as a China Correspondent. I remained there for two years—witnessing the social upheaval that resulted in the Tiananmen Square uprising and military crackdown. I was evacuated on the last U.S. flight out of Beijing in the chaos following the Tiananmen massacre and took R&R for two weeks before returning to Beijing. I stayed there for a few more months under the Chinese government's military repression before deciding it would be nice to return to California

I work at my desk at The Journal of Commerce office in Hong Kong.

and live again on American soil.

The words that follow are mine based on my experiences in China at what would become a pivotal point in history. Pseudonyms have been substituted for the names of living people. Some of my former colleagues have since passed away so I mention them by name—like my dear old editor Phil from Buffalo, New York.

I became an expert financial journalist thanks to Phil. He had every confidence in my abilities even though I'd had little prior experience reporting on commodities, banking, businesses, economics, etc. He decided to hire me after a chance introduction at the FCC, a place he rarely ventured out to.

I had been covering criminal and civil courts for the English newspaper in Hong Kong which was read by educated Chinese. (The competing *South China Morning Post* was for the expat crowd.) My newspaper office at the *HongKong Standard* was located on the mainland far away from the Hong Kong Island expat set. It was staffed by mostly Hong Kong Chinese reporters, and our editor was veteran newsman Henry Parwani—who gained fame after breaking news about the death of martial arts superstar Bruce Lee in 1973.

Since I was working for a newspaper in Hong Kong, I wasn't considered a "foreign correspondent." But Phil offered me a chance to become one. He called me "Lovey" as he did all women he liked. Once I moved to China, he jokingly called me the "Beijing Belle" or "Belle". I didn't see it as sexist and felt no offense. He was a warm-hearted guy who had been with United Press International for years—a former "Unipresser". I had never even read the business section of a newspaper before I took the JOC job. It reminds me of the time I bought a car as a teen without knowing how to drive one. Necessity is a powerful motivator. I learned in a day how to handle that Ford Fairmont's stick shift and learned in a week about business news after reading articles with a dictionary. Phil was content to pad around the JOC office in a rumpled sweater and in his stocking feet (shoes off) inside a top floor of a swank modern building in the Central District of Hong Kong. Reuters was located a few floors down on the same elevator ride. I was to be the roving foreign correspondent, while Phil edited articles and sent them to the foreign desk in New York City. It was the days of early computers, portable typewriters, telexes, and newfangled fax machines. When I went on the road in Asia, I took my typewriter and sent my stories via telex to Hong Kong. Once in China, I filed my stories through a

Philip (P.T.) Bangsberg, my editor, in the Hong Kong office of The Journal of Commerce. A native of New York, Phil was one of the most gifted editors I ever worked with. He began his news career as a teen working in radio. He worked at UPI, ABC News Radio and The New York Times before moving to London, where he was the foreign copy editor at The Daily Telegraph. Then he was deputy night editor for The Times of London. He became managing editor for the Birmingham Evening Mail. Upon arriving in Asia, he joined the South China Morning Post as deputy business editor before jumping to the JOC. Always calm under pressure, he wrote with an easy wit and great flair. His editing was like fine-tuning my work. Some editors replace your voice in writing with their own — not Phil. My reflection appears in the lower photo.

During my first year as a foreign correspondent covering Asia and China, I'm sitting at my desk in the JOC newsroom in Hong Kong.

wire service.

It's easy to have an enlarged ego when you're a foreign correspondent. Your job is to tell what's important in another country and report on it for the eyes of thousands of readers across the globe. You may be a nobody in your own country, but you can make a president of another country hear you and respond to your questions. Quite an ego rush for some people to level that kind of playing field!

Many foreign correspondents I've known in Asia and Europe sit in their comfy offices and monitor foreign news reports, which they sift through to repeat almost verbatim or put their "expert" spin on it. They rarely get out among the people to hear what others have to say, rarely leave the capital city where most are based, and rarely have an open mind to learn from the people and places around them. Instead often they occupy lofty seats to look down with jaded eyes upon the "locals" and pal around with other foreigners, their own countrymen, and select diplomats. Insular experiences can result in the shaping of distorted news that becomes a "follow-the-pack" type of journalism. Obviously this generalization isn't true of everyone. And, I count myself among the foreign correspondents who like to explore the surrounding world and learn from encounters with others.

So that's what you'll find in the following pages—remembrances of my time as a young American woman journalist experiencing a very different world from one I'd ever known before.

Part 2: Travels into China as a Foreign Correspondent

Chapter 2:
The First 30 Days

I board a Dragonair flight in Thailand during my days as a foreign correspondent in Asia.

As I prepared to take my first trip from Hong Kong into China, I recall watching television in July 1986 to view the wedding of Prince Andrew and Sarah Ferguson. The much-anticipated event was a welcome relief from my worries as I packed my belongings in a suitcase. I was 27 years old.

I began my journalism studies at the University of New Mexico in the days when it had a Journalism Department. The Journalism school was very proud of its hometown hero, World War II war correspondent Ernie Pyle, who chose Albuquerque as the place to build his dream home in 1940. Pyle lived in his beloved house located only one mile away from the Journalism Department at UNM.

In keeping with the standards of Pulitzer-Prize-winning Pyle, the UNM Journalism School hired notable faculty who formed me as a journalist. My two most influential professors were news veterans.

- *Margaret Hyman*—a former UPI Bureau Chief in Puerto Rico, she began her career as a newspaper woman after graduating from Northwestern University in 1955. She obtained a rare interview with Nathan Leopold a year before he died. Leopold and his pal Richard Loeb together committed a nationally sensational crime in 1924 when they murdered a boy in an experiment. Alfred Hitchcock made a movie based on the Leopold and Loeb crime. A tiny woman who dressed with feminine flair, Professor Hyman had a fiery personality. She was one of the few women in journalism who at that time (or since then) wasn't competitive with me nor insecurely threatened by me. Instead she acted like a mentor, encouraging me to have high standards in my news reporting and be the best I could be. I knew her when she was dying of cancer. A chain-smoker, she always wore a smile and never let on about her medical condition. She was tough. And also one of the kindest women I've ever met. She cared about her students and journalism, ensuring the next generation of reporters, editors and photographers would be instilled with the same high commitment to serving society. She encouraged me to be confident being the woman I was as I entered a man's world in the news business (rather than trying to mold myself into something else to fit in).

- *Stuart Novins*—a CBS news legend, Professor Novins joined CBS Radio during World War II as a war reporter in Europe with his buddies Edward R. Murrow and Eric Sevareid. Novins made history in his career. He was one of three journalists on the panel during the 1960 presidential debate between Richard Nixon and John F. Kennedy. He was a Tokyo bureau chief and correspondent for the United Nations and Latin America. He became the 2nd moderator for "Face the Nation," which today is among the longest-airing news shows in history. A former Moscow bureau chief from 1962–1965, Novins was one of three journalists to conduct a ground-breaking interview with Soviet leader Nikita Khrushchev. For seven years, Novins anchored CBS

News Radio broadcasts before retiring to New Mexico to teach journalism students, including me, at UNM.

Novins had a great impact on my way of thinking and the journalist I became. Although also a friend of Walter Cronkite, he spoke to us mostly about Murrow. He had high expectations for his students.

We had to follow in the footsteps of the journalism giant Edward R. Murrow. He told us we had a duty as journalists. We had to get it right or get out. We had to be objective or get out. We had to evaluate the information we received in our interviews/reporting with personal responsibility for its publication or dissemination on the airwaves. We couldn't just say something because someone told it to us. That was wrong. We had to take a hard look at what we were told and who told it to us. We had to evaluate the credibility of our information and its newsworthiness. One factual error on any news article we wrote meant an automatic F for that assignment. If any of us students got at total of three F's, we were automatically expelled from his class.

He detested journalism that combined opinion with fact.

"A free people, in order to remain free, must know," he declared.

It was either straight, hard news or an opinion piece. He didn't even like it when TV and radio newscasters introduced commercial sponsors. He said that tarnished their impartiality and all-important credibility with the public. He drilled it into us that we were to be objective. If we had an opinion, we were to keep it to ourselves. He told us we had to be prepared to make personal sacrifices as journalists. He said we should never register under any political party. How could we ever cover politics with any semblance of impartiality if we were registered to vote under a political party or if we gave money to any organization or cause? We had to forego voting in primary elections (where a person's vote can count the most in a presidential election) since we could not belong to a political party. Instead, we were instructed to register to vote as "undeclared." He told us never to be intimidated when interviewing anyone no matter how high a person's status or rank. All people are only human. I followed his inspiring advice.

When I look at the mandate in today's world by some news organizations for their reporters to have social media accounts (publicizing their journalism jobs) to pronounce their views and share content from others (often indicating endorsements), I think back to Stuart Novins. I wonder what he would think today about the status of what he viewed as the noblest of professions—journalism.

This photo of me was taken while I was college student learning to be a journalist at UNM.

How does what we see cloaked as "news" by "journalists" jive with his mandate that a journalist should strive to be objective, not blur facts with opinions, and maintain the impartial integrity of the noble profession of journalism?

Novins encouraged my class of young journalists to aspire to walk in the footsteps of his friend and longtime CBS colleague Edward R. Murrow. What would Murrow—known for his integrity and hailed as one of the world's finest journalists in modern history—think about today's crop of journalists?

In my junior year, I transferred to San Francisco State University's journalism program, which also had notable journalism professors there. But none had the same impact on me as Novins and Hyman. The training I had in both J-schools isn't really done today. There is a greater current emphasis on technology, multimedia, digital reporting and communications. Often communications programs are blended with journalism.

In my educational formation, I had a heavy emphasis on writing, including how to cover an event in multiple ways/different angles. We had to learn about the different types of news articles. One of my first assignments in news-writing class called for us students to write our own obituaries. Most of us were teens and intensely disliked this assignment to ponder our demise. Who wants to think about dying at that age? We had to figure out our cause of death, survivors, funeral arrangements, etc. All the elements about what we would have to ask when interviewing and writing an obituary had to be included in our assignment.

We also had to write "brights"—short articles on cheerful subjects.

Then there was the inverted pyramid format for news with the most important information on top and the least at the end so it could be cut to fit within a given space in layout.

There were "man-on-the-street" articles, which are no fun at all. You stand somewhere and grab ordinary people to interview in order to get a general view about something. Breaking news. Second-day news of an event. Next came different types of feature articles, editorial opinion and analysis pieces. Magazine writing, which provides a more literary format than the confines of a newspaper. Getting a journalism degree required lots of editing classes, and learning writing styles and headlines. How do you use hyphens, serial commas? Which numbers are spelled out? Which states are abbreviated? How do you write lists of data from public records?

We also had to take classes on law—especially libel, privacy, and defamation. Not only were we required to know about the law to cover it, but we had to learn what information was public and what we shouldn't print about people and companies. For instance, who is a public figure? What can you say about them in the news? Other requirements were to learn about Freedom of the Press, the People's Right to Know, and journalism history. A significant amount of attention was

My graduation ceremony in San Francisco where I earned a B.A. in Journalism.

paid to the penny press of the 1830s (in which news became available to ordinary people), yellow journalism of William Randolph Hearst (the worst type of manipulation of so-called news), and mass communication (radio, TV). I don't think the same amount of academic rigor is applied to today's journalism school graduates.

If a foreign correspondent has this type of educational formation in journalism and experience-based knowledge from rising through the ranks of news, he or she will be a much different journalist than someone who becomes a foreign correspondent mostly based on the academic ability to speak a foreign language or catapulted from a posh school to a posh job with little news experience.

I'd become hooked on journalism at once in college when I took my first news writing class at age 19. I was so enthusiastic that I wrote news articles for extra credit by interviewing local officials, such as city firemen, to gain real-world experience in journalism. I wanted to be a TV reporter but the university only offered a program for print news. So, my formal education was as a print journalist with photojournalism courses. However I worked hard independently, gaining internships in broadcast news to learn the business by actually doing it as an unpaid volunteer. At the same time, I supported myself and paid for my own education. It was not easy. My grades were okay, but never great even though I was considered a gifted student. I never had the luxury of solely devoting myself to my education. I had to earn the money to pay for it, plus books and living expenses. At the same time, I had to gain expertise so I could hit the ground running in the news business by the time I graduated.

While in college, I worked my way up the intern ladder from writing radio news to TV news reporting. I had an internship at KTVU in Oakland, then the 5th largest (San Francisco Bay area) television viewing market in the nation, which meant there were high standards for journalism and high expectations for work performance. One day the TV news producer tossed some blank script pages at myself and two other interns. He asked us to write a news piece. After I turned mine in, he frowned as he read it. Looking up, he asked: "Can you do it again?" I said, "Sure." I wrote another one. He read it, tossed me another blank page, scribbled some info down and told me to do some interviews and write another script like I was on deadline. I did and handed my script to him 15 minutes later.

From then on, I was a professional TV news writer throughout the rest of my college days and for a couple months after I graduated at age 23. I wrote news and also worked on the assignment desk giving reporters information for news stories (packages). I was on the brink of getting hired full-time when one of guys on the assignment desk threatened me, trying to coerce me to sleep with him if I wanted to get hired. He told me I had a week to think it over. At the end of the week, I phoned him and told him, "No". I was never called to work again-either to write the 10 p.m. newscast or help out on the assignment desk. In fact, I was unable to get a job in TV news at all. I don't know if it was because I listed that TV station as a reference for my work experience. I thought perhaps I'd been blackballed.

I quickly realized that I needed to rely on my training and education as a newspaper reporter if I was to remain a journalist. Acting quickly, I found a short-term unpaid job for a couple days a week as a reporter for the *Millbrae Sun* newspaper, located about 15 miles south of San Francisco. I needed clips (newspaper clippings of my

Since international time zones were critical for deadlines, clocks in our Hong Kong newsroom showed the time in key locations.

articles) to show potential employers. I had some clips from the student newspaper (the *Golden Gater*) where I had been a reporter covering the university police beat at San Francisco State University.

I had made a good name for myself covering a series of campus rapes and subsequent trial of the alleged rapist. As each attack became more violent and twisted, university police feared the assailant would turn to killing women. Local San Francisco news organizations took notice and began covering the attacks by the serial rapist. Although I broke news in my campus articles, I could get a job easier if I had clips from a regular newspaper. So I contacted local papers to see if I could find a way to work as a reporter. The *Millbrae Sun* didn't refuse my offer.

After I started as a general assignment reporter, the publisher called me into his office to set me straight about me how things worked there. He told me I could write anything I wanted about police, the community and politics, but I was to stay a million miles away from writing anything negative about the Lions Club or any local companies run by Lions. "What? You've got to be kidding," I thought. I didn't even really know—or care—about the Lions Club. So much for all those fine journalism principles instilled in me during my university classes about the profession involving "the People's Right to Know," I mused. This is real life.

Another memorable incident of my time at the *Millbrae Sun* involved a sadistic police chief. Unlike many recent college grads from J-school, I'd already covered a significant amount of police and court-related news for professional news organizations where I had worked. I knew my way around what documents I was entitled to obtain as public records and how not to be jerked around by police who tried to hide information using the "it's under investigation" mantra. I also knew that some officers could be sexist jerks, but most were not. To be successful on the police beat, you had to win respect. There were two main rules. First, you had to be careful to get the facts right. Secondly, you didn't burn your sources when they provided you with or allowed you to see confidential info to help you understand the big picture of what they really thought was going on. That respect had to be mutual—without the police pulling any funny business on me. If they pulled any tricks on me or tried anything underhanded, I'd have an adversarial relationship with them all the way.

I knocked heads with the Millbrae police chief after my first interview with him. A body had been discovered in the San Francisco Bay, and I wanted to write about it. I was ushered into his office. Nothing unusual. Sometimes the big cheeses in an organization want to see their names in print and be the only source quoted in the newspaper. I took my seat after the introductions. I whipped out my reporter's notebook and started asking questions. He wore a smirk the entire time. Then he handed me a folder with information for me to view. I opened it and saw a series of close-up photos of the disintegrated face of what had once been a person. It was impossible to tell if it was a man or woman after it had been in the water for at least three months. He chuckled and waited to see if I'd react squeamishly. I didn't. I wouldn't give him the satisfaction of a sensitive reaction. I finished the interview, knowing I was dealing with a first-class jerk! I didn't work long in Millbrae. I think I lasted a few weeks. I left one day, not bothering to return. It wasn't worth my time.

Shortly afterwards, I got my first real newspaper job

While covering the police beat in Palm Springs and Desert Hot Springs for The Desert Sun newspaper, I interviewed members of the notorious Vagos Motorcycle Club. Puff (left) was a locksmith.

working for an influential Chinese family (the Fangs) at *AsianWeek* newspaper in Chinatown, San Francisco. I was one of only two non-Asians at the weekly newspaper. It was a terrific experience. I came to know and respect the Fang family, particularly my boss John Fang (T.C. Fong) and his elegant wife, who operated a restaurant on Grant Avenue. One of their three sons assisted with the newspaper. Often Mr. Fang, a newspaperman from Shanghai, had me attend luncheon meetings over dim sum at the family restaurant. Other times, he had me run errands in Chinatown where I got to meet his cronies. He didn't limit my job duties to journalism, since he viewed all his employees as working for his family. Many times, I came to work in the morning to find a Chinese treat (like a steamed pork bun) on my desk. I honed my journalism skills at the same time I gained my first experience working within a Chinese culture. The Fang family, always hardworking and involved in their community, went onto make journalism history with their purchase of the *San Francisco Examiner* newspaper.

During my time at *AsianWeek*, I also learned more about the diversity of different groups. The editorial mandate of the newspaper was to give a voice in articles and opinion pieces to different Asian groups, including the Japanese and Filipinos. One of the columnists I came to know was Lim P. Lee, a former Postmaster of San Francisco and Democratic powerhouse in local and state politics.

After *AsianWeek*, I worked for a daily newspaper in Palm Springs—*The Desert Sun* newspaper, which was bought by

Gannett during my time there. I covered a variety of news beats and cities (including Cathedral City and Desert Hot Springs) for over a year before moving up to focus on the police beat (cops and courts) in Palm Springs.

While at *AsianWeek*, I had heard people there talk about wild and wicked Hong Kong, which I thought sounded exotic and intriguing. During those days, I once sat on a plane next to a Navy sailor, who described his travels. He declared that Hong Kong was his favorite place. Fate would point me to Hong Kong and China during a dinner in Palm Springs when I sat next to a British journalist named Ian Markham-Smith. A former Fleet Street journalist, Ian had worked in Hong Kong. I asked him some questions about Hong Kong over a lively dinner with lots of drinking. At the end of that evening's merriment, Ian had given me the names of three journalists in Hong Kong, and I'd drunkenly decided there and then that Hong Kong would be the next stop in my journalism career.

One of my most popular feature articles, from July 19, 1985, when I was a reporter at The Desert Sun newspaper in Palm Springs, California.

The next morning, I sobered up and thought, "What the heck? Why not?" A few months later, I had sold my Ford Fairmont, bought a round-trip plane ticket, been vaccinated, bid my farewells and landed at Kai Tak Airport with a couple of hundred dollars in my hand, no prebooked hotel, and a suitcase. Two weeks later, I landed my job at the *HongKong*

Sights from my taxi ride in Guangzhou (Canton). Photos by Noël-Marie Fletcher.

Standard. Then Phil gave me the chance to show what I was made of—and I certainly did.

On my first trip to the mainland, the train to China left at Kowloon (Nine Dragons) on the peninsula for a two-hour trip to Shenzhen, which had created a Special Economic Zone with business incentives. I remember the upholstered seats on the train had beautiful white crocheted lace draped over the headrests. The Chinese authorities looked over my passport and papers when I crossed over the border. I admit I was very anxious and somewhat scared. I didn't know what to expect being required to go many places in a strange country where I didn't speak the language. Also for this trip into China, I'd have to travel to different cities using different modes of transportation. And, finally, I was to be there for 30 days, which is a long business trip by any definition.

My interviews with Chinese-owned companies were all structured the same way. The only thing that differed were the sizes of the entourages. Sometimes there could be at least a dozen people, including the drivers, who sat in during my interviews. I was the lone foreigner amid a group of mostly Chinese men. Some wore Western-style clothes and others, particularly if representing the Communist party, wore Chinese clothing (the blue collared jackets, blue caps and round cloth shoes). For each company, there were two main spokesmen—a member of the Communist Party (political) leader and a business person who actually managed day-to-day operations. The party member often tried to take over conversations but lacked the details I needed in response to my questions. That's when the business manager would step in to answer my questions. For interviews, I always used an interpreter, provided by the company or myself.

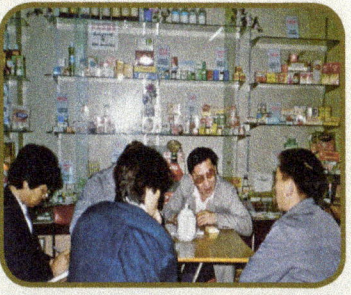

My journalism interviews in Guangzhou with Chinese businessmen. Top: A traditional Chinese medicine company, with a showroom sign saying: "Development of New Commodities." Center: Meeting site. Bottom: Glove and belt makers. Photos by Noël-Marie Fletcher.

Some reporters relied on tape recorders, while others used notebooks. Like most who use notebooks, I developed my own shorthand, which was very accurate. The only time ever I brought a tape recorder was when interviewing a difficult person. I would want the person to know that everything was recorded to avoid any accusation of being misquoted—usually I'd use a tape recorder to intimidate the subject or provide protection insurance for myself. Even then, I took notes and verified the accuracy of my writing against a transcript of the tape.

In China, I sat at a place of honor next to the pair of main interviewees. The interpreter always sat next to me. I learned my first sayings in Mandarin from hearing the repetition of phrases from interpreters during the interviews. Sometimes I had nonstop meetings (up to four in a day). At night, my dreams many times were in Mandarin since I'd been listening to it all day long.

The rooms for the interviews were always arranged with couches and chairs in rectangles around a table. Hot Chinese tea was always served. Small end tables were placed between the couches. If a room was large enough, it could have interior rings of couches or chairs. Large ashtrays sat on all tables. Chinese men were heavy smokers.

A Chinese official wears a traditional Mao suit stands during an interview on economic development. Photo by Noël-Marie Fletcher.

I also enjoyed smoking back then. The men were always surprised when I'd take my pack of menthol cigarettes out and place them on a table in front of me next to my purse. My cigarettes were thin and dark like a cigar, which also caused them curiosity. I was a double novelty: a female smoker and a young American woman. If I got along well with the people I was interviewing, we'd trade cigarettes, smoke them together and laughingly make comparisons. They always had Chinese brands, like Double Happiness. At meals, an ashtray was arranged between each place setting. Like my Chinese hosts, I'd smoke during meals while different platters of dishes were prepared and served in intervals. I shared lots of laughs trading cigarettes with the men. Theirs were always stronger and harsher than mine. They'd be polite and light my cigarette. Then I'd return the favor to light theirs. I'm sure they found me bold but I didn't mind. The only people present who seemed to disapprove of me were older frowning Chinese women occasionally present in the groups. The younger Chinese women usually didn't show any resentment or disapproval even though they didn't partake in smoking cigarettes.

The first morning interview would drag out to include a mandatory luncheon. As the guest of honor, I sat next to the host, who gave me deferential treatment. No one else would take a bite from a dish until I did.

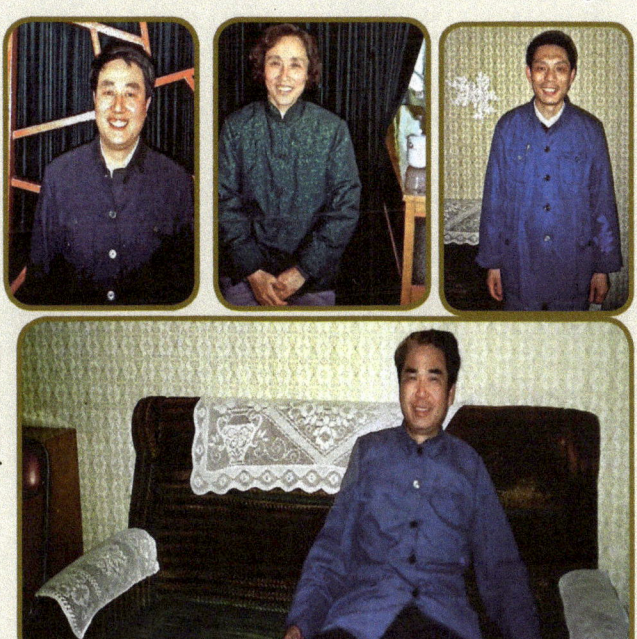

Many of business leaders I spoke with wore the traditional Chinese blue suits and jackets. Photos by Noël-Marie Fletcher.

I learned to bury food I didn't want to eat in my rice bowl. I'd push it with the chopsticks to the bottom of my bowl and take some rice to eat. I soon learned that the companies would serve delicacies for lunch that ordinary Chinese people ate infrequently. Many times, this food appealed more to their tastes than my foreign ones. Although I like hot spicy food, I'm not an adventurous eater. I like my steak well done. I enjoy basic Chinese food, Indian cuisine, and Thai dishes. But I'll take a pass on certain exotic foods—including such delicacies in southern China as pigeon, abalone, toad (which they referred to as a "field chicken"), thousand-year-old eggs, duck tongues, and sea cucumbers (phallic-looking marine animals). Many Cantonese people laughingly told me a humorous proverbial saying that they eat anything in the sky except airplanes, anything underwater except submarines, and anything on land

Above, below and opposite page: Pairs of Chinese business officials pose after being interviewed. Usually one was in charge of business operations and the other with Communist activities within a company. Photos (both pages) by Noël-Marie Fletcher.

with four legs except tables.

I found an interpreter in Guangzhou who I began to rely on. She was very good. A young wife, she worked for the government. When I'd come into town, I'd arrange for her to help me in my interviews. I always took her out to lunch and dinner at nice restaurants to express my thanks. She was crazy about eating pigeon. She'd always order a whole one, with its head included on the side as was customary. I'd order my favorite dishes, too. We both loved hot corn egg-drop soup. When it was time for desert, we also liked sago soup (a cold tapioca-type dish). I liked her and wanted to reward her for her much-appreciated assistance. She took great pride in her work.

Some translators were unhelpful. For example, sometimes a Chinese businessman would reply to my question with a long response taking several minutes. A disinterested translator would turn to me with a one-sentence reply. I knew there was no way that the short answer was a translation of the entire response. I'd push back on the translator to tell me exactly a word-for-word response.

Most Chinese translators decided whether they wanted to choose to speak English with a British or American accent. From what I was told, it was a big decision. Most opted to have a British accent. It they had an American accent, they tended to work mostly with Americans in U.S. joint-venture companies or news organizations.

My travels included skimming atop the South China Sea inside a hydrofoil (a jet-propelled catamaran). The vessels provided a high-speed way to shoot across the waters in a comfortable environment. Tourists and business travelers filled the boats, which were expensive passenger options. I preferred hydrofoils to trains and flying. It was great to be on the open sea, with terrific scenic views, while shooting across the water. The interiors were air-conditioned, roomy and had better seating than ferry boats. I also rode in hydrofoils for weekend jaunts from Hong Kong to Macau, then still a Portuguese colony at one tip of mainland China near the Pearl River Delta. I always had a great time in Macau, known for its gambling dens (of which I didn't partake). I enjoyed the scenic colorful housing in Macau (pastel greens and yellows) and loved Portuguese cuisine—especially the spicy food (such as African chicken), green wine (Vinho Verde), and olive oil. Years later when making business trips to Newark,

New Jersey, I made a point of dining in Portuguese restaurants to enjoy my favorites dishes and drinks I recalled from my time in Macau.

Ruins of St. Paul's Church, built by the Jesuits in the early 1600s in Macau (left); a lamppost with a sign in Portuguese, English and Chinese. Photos by Noël-Marie Fletcher.

One of my favorite memories of Macau was staying at an old Portuguese colonial hotel near the waterfront. It had a wide verandah where I spent an enjoyable weekend basking in the warm sunlight while drinking pastis. I returned to the hotel late one evening, disturbing an elderly Chinese watchman, who made nasty faces at me as he opened the door to let me inside. I looked down at his feet and noticed he wore a pair of traditional black cloth shoes with a V-opening. I had seen black cloth martial arts shoes but none like this. I loved the look. Since my shoe size was a large as an average Chinese man's foot, I had no trouble finding a pair in a Chinese market. The shoes became my favorite go-to shoe during my time in China. I also enjoyed wearing women's and men's Chinese-style sweaters and cotton shirts with frog buttons. I bought those at mainland stores. In

Views of Macau. Photos by Noël-Marie Fletcher.

Shanghai, I bought several cheongsam (*qipao*) dresses made of silk (bright yellow and in royal blue) and maroon velvet. I noticed that Chinese people would react in surprise when I wore the clothes. I was very thin and received many compliments from Chinese people when I wore the cheongsam dresses. I wore one once to a wedding of a Belgian journalist friend of mine who married a Hong Kong Chinese woman.

I bought some velvet Chinese cheongsams (like the one I'm holding above). A mainland clothing department, photo below by Noël-Marie Fletcher.

The only hostility or negativity I received was from British expatriates, who gave me sourly disapproving looks and made negative facial expressions.

I think today's recent controversy of over purported "culture appropriation" of a non-Chinese woman wearing a cheongsam is ridiculous. To me, this is a form of racial bullying. People are entitled to wear whatever they like. Such thinking is as ludicrous as saying that a Chinese person should only use chopsticks rather than a knife and fork. Or that only men should be allowed to wear pants. Why put people in a box or slap a label on them? People should be free to express themselves in their choices of clothing. When I wore Chinese clothing, I wore it because I liked it—a form of cultural appreciation.

Macau was also the site of one of my most shameful memories. I had been taken there for a few days by some foreign journalist acquaintances, who wanted to show me around since I was a newbie in Asia. We rented a vehicle and drove around exploring.

One place was a leper colony in Ka Ho village on Coloane Island. Its buildings dated back to the late 1800s. My guides told me we could drive through the village and, if we were lucky, see a leper. I'm ashamed to say that at the time, I found this rather exciting. We drove through the entire village. I was struck by how neat and clean everything was in the houses and yards. There were carefully tended shrines to the Blessed Virgin Mary in some outdoor areas.

Street scenes in China showed the hard life some people led. Photos by Noël-Marie Fletcher.

We became very frustrated since we couldn't see anyone. Eventually, we stopped driving and got out at a church. We went inside. When I saw large metal cans of disinfectant everywhere, I became fearful about catching the disease. I wanted to leave immediately. I wasted no time in exiting through the doorway. As I did, I nearly bumped into an aged Chinese woman wearing a broad-brimmed circular hat with a point; it was made of bamboo. As she looked up at me, glaring in disapproval, I saw she had no nose. She looked straight into my eyes as if saying, "Is this what you want to see? Well, take a look!"

I felt as low as a worm. I was so ashamed of myself for thinking of those poor people as some sort of freak-show amusement. I jumped back into the vehicle and wanted to leave immediately.

The Pearl River Delta. Photo by Noël-Marie Fletcher.

I don't recall any of my companions sharing in my remorse. To this day, I regard that experience with regret even though the leper colony is long gone. Back then, Macau also was in its last colonial days. It returned to China in 1999. As with Hong Kong, I was a witness to its last era of time under European control.

After I left Shenzhen during my first foray into China, I went to Guangzhou (Canton) on the Pearl River Delta, which flows into the South China Sea. I expected the famed waterway to be picturesque and pristine. Instead, it looked like the brownest and darkest muddy waters I'd ever seen. I thought it looked like a contaminated place to be avoided rather than anything resembling a lustrous pearl.

I enjoyed the hustle and bustle of Guangzhou. I interviewed many sharp Chinese business officials. They seemed to be not only very experienced in dealing with foreign ventures but adept at knowing exactly what they wanted to receive from capitalistic countries. In some areas I later visited in China, the businessmen acted like they had no clue what they were doing, but were rather trying to figure it out as they went along. The people of Guangzhou were very proud of being

A Chinese company official paused after my interview for a photo. Photo by Noël-Marie Fletcher.

The manager of a battery factory, shown at the bottom. The showroom (middle) had samples. Photos by Noël-Marie Fletcher.

Cantonese. Although Mandarin was the official language, they made it perfectly clear they preferred to speak in Cantonese. So all my interpreters avoided having conversations in Mandarin, and my interview questions and answers were in the local Cantonese dialect.

I'll never forget my experiences at mainland airports during my domestic travels. Guangzhou was my initiation. My Mandarin was very poor during my early travels in China. I bought a tourist phrase book in pinyin that showed the words in Roman letters with accent marks

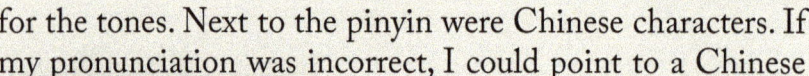

for the tones. Next to the pinyin were Chinese characters. If my pronunciation was incorrect, I could point to a Chinese

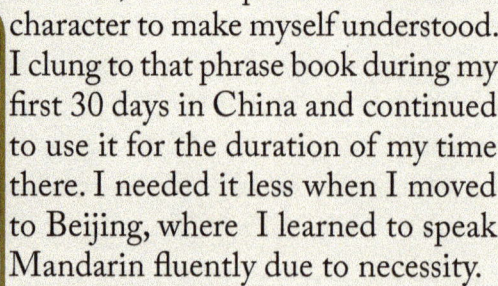

character to make myself understood. I clung to that phrase book during my first 30 days in China and continued to use it for the duration of my time there. I needed it less when I moved to Beijing, where I learned to speak Mandarin fluently due to necessity.

After the taxi picked me up at my hotel and brought me to the Guangzhou airport, I made my way to the China Airlines section. I don't recall which city I was flying to in the hinterland. The room was crowded with people everywhere. I was the only foreigner in sight. I found an airline worker, who explained with irritation that I was supposed to look at a chalkboard on the wall for my flight number. This was difficult. I could only recognize numerals since everything else was written in Chinese characters. I had to keep sight of the number of my plane. I couldn't understand anything being spoken around me nor any airport announcements being made.

Chinese hospitality for me as a foreign journalist included beer and a platter of crab at a banquet. Photo by Noël-Marie Fletcher.

After an hour or so waiting in the lobby, I saw people pointing to the same number as my airplane. I figured out they were also passengers, and it was time to depart. I followed them until I found another airline worker who spoke English. She confirmed my flight was indeed ready to depart. She told me to follow the people onto the tarmac to find the number painted on the airplane and board it. I couldn't believe it. I joined everyone going out and wandering on the tarmac—scrutinizing the planes as if they were cars in a parking lot. We were all looking for the numbers painted on

Bicycles, large trucks (center) and carts driven by horses, donkeys and mules were common sights in China. Photo by Noël-Marie Fletcher.

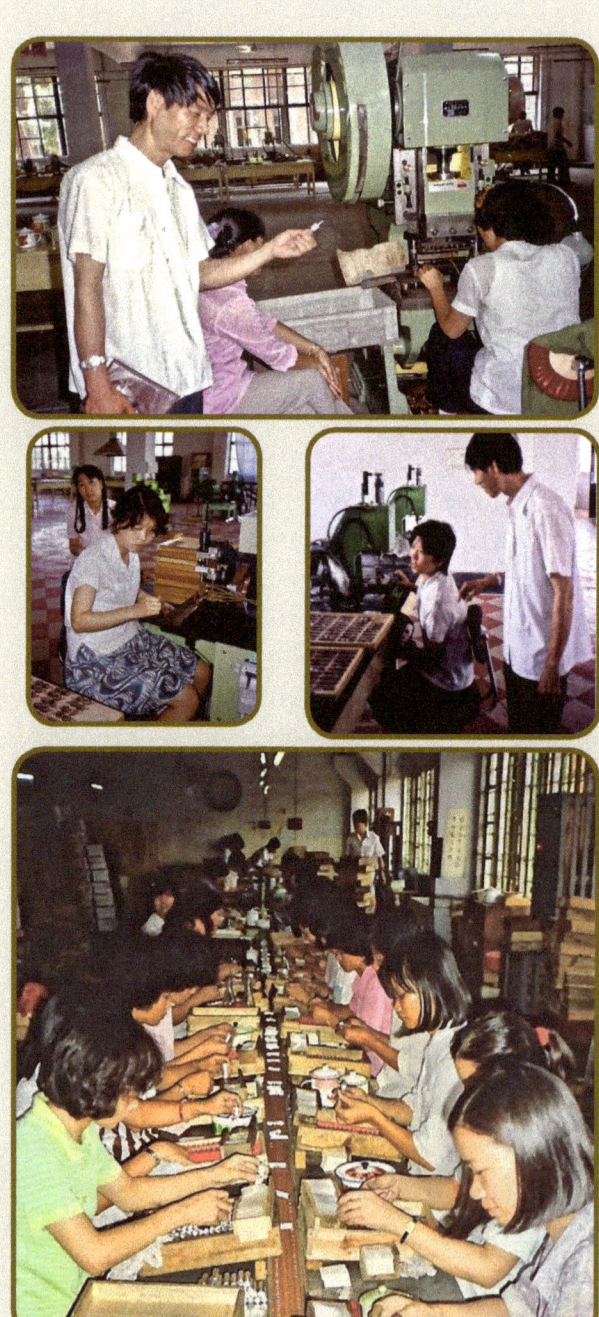

A typical journalist interview included a tour at a Chinese factory followed by a banquet meal at the company. Photos (above) by Noël-Marie Fletcher.

the bodies of the airplanes. Once we found the correct number, we climbed up the stairs to board the flight.

The flight experiences in mainland China were

I was the only woman in the group and waited to share lunch after my interview.

unlike what I was used to in Hong Kong, in other Asian countries, or in the United States. People didn't use the seat belts if they didn't feel like it. Stewardesses didn't seem to care either. Some seats didn't work properly—reclining backwards or forwards. Tray tables were also sometimes permanently down. When it was time for a snack, stewardesses would toss dripping cardboard boxes (made with low-quality, razor-thin paper material) out to the passengers as if dealing cards from a deck. After passengers ate their dripping food, the boxes were cast onto the floor sometimes for the duration of the flight.

Souvenirs were also distributed. I amassed quite a collection of paper fans from my airplane travels, which came in handy during hot summer days. I still have a number of them.

When I think of the stewardesses, I recall surly faces and grumpy demeanors. The customer-is-always-right notion and desire for top customer service were not part of Chinese Communist workers' culture that I experienced. Another novel part of air travel I soon became accustomed to was a general grooming practice of clipping fingernails and toenails. The click-click-click of nail clippers became a common background noise during flights. I often saw people working on their fingernails from the comfort of their seats. Occasionally, I witnessed some passengers take off their socks and hoist a foot up, cross-legged, to attended to

A Chinese boat sails in the background as chefs in a mainland hotel prepare lunch. Photo by Noël-Marie Fletcher.

the pruning. I cringed, wondering what direction the nail tips would fly once they snapped off.

The display of a bad attitude towards airline passengers was also shared by many airport employees who inspected luggage for departures. Once I had a good laugh at two such airport officials. They were being snide and giving me a hard time as they inspected my belongings before a departure. I liked to collect examples of items made by local artisans during my trips to China. On that particular trip, I had a large cardboard box containing a life-sized replica of a terracotta warrior's head. Struggling with my luggage, purse and collectibles in tow, I resented what I thought was harassment from those two rogues. One picked up the heavy cardboard box and snickered as he started to open it. Parting the shreds of newspaper surrounding a gray unfinished ceramic object, the official gasped and nearly dropped the box. He had reached in and thought he was pulling

The replica head of the terracotta warrior on my desk in Beijing. Photo by Noël-Marie Fletcher.

out a decapitated head. I started laughing and showed him the replica of the warrior's head, which had very lifelike facial features and hair tied upswept in a topknot. He was done with me. I was free to go. I don't know if he was superstitious or not. He wanted me and my belongings out of there. I was only too glad to comply.

A train station in China. Photo by Noël-Marie Fletcher.

Another memorable experience from my first trip into China involved an overnight train trip from southern China to the famous and picturesque eastern city of Hangzhou (Hangchow). My train travel had been quite limited at that point. I'd only traveled short distances during the daytime. For my travel attire, I relied on jeans as well as denim or khaki dresses that needed no ironing. I could look presentable while wearing more rugged clothing. For that trip, I wore my calf-length khaki dress with a wide cloth belt and deep pockets that I could fill with any items I needed.

With a suitcase and portable typewriter in hand, I boarded the train and took my seat in an overnight compartment. It had four bench-like beds (two on each side). I was alone and sat on a lower bench. My mind wandered as I looked out the window while watching the comings and goings of people on the rail platform. A little while later, a man came into the compartment. I thought, "Okay, this is a bit weird." Never having been in a sleeper car, I had no idea what to expect. But the thought of sharing that compartment with a strange guy was uncomfortable. Before long, two more men joined us. I jumped up to the top bench and wondered about my safety sleeping in this railway car with three strange men. I spoke no Chinese and said nothing. Instead, I pulled my belongings close to me and sat there staring at them from above. They appeared to be just as uncomfortable as I was, which I took to be a good sign. They muttered among themselves as I watched them intently for a while. I wondered if any of those men would get any unwelcome ideas about me being in there alone with them.

Soon afterwards, the train departed. A woman train attendant came into our railcar. She acted nonchalant about all of us being in the same car as she checked our tickets. I thought that was another positive sign. I decided it would be best for me to stay right where I was and sleep in my clothes. I tried to stay awake as long as possible. Finally unable to keep my eyes open, I fell asleep. During my slumber, I recall the forward chugging motion of the train as it continued the journey with stops in between. I briefly awoke in the darkness to the sound of screaming pigs being herded through some station during a stop. The shrill squeals and grunting sounded like the pigs were being prepared for railway transport. Despite my head being heavy with sleep, I recall thinking what an odd experience I was having as I rolled over onto my side. The next morning, I jumped upright, fully clothed and wearing my boots, ready to arrive in Hangzhou.

Sampans in Cheung Chau harbor. Photos by Noël-Marie Fletcher.

Recalling that awful din from what sounded like hundreds of pigs brings to mind another unexpected and disturbing pig memory. For most of my time in Hong Kong, I lived on an idyllic fishing island named Cheung Chau some six miles southwest of Hong Kong. Only accessible by ferry, there were no cars on the tropical island. Like the other odd assortment of some 30 foreigners living there, I had a flat on the top of the island overlooking the Chinese villagers and fishing families who lived in junks and other boats. Sampans bobbed up and down the harbor relaying people to other boats as well as to the shore. The ferryboat came every hour or so and stopped running around 10 p.m. Because the island had no streetlights, I had to bring a flashlight (or

The first place I lived in Hong Kong was on the fishing island of Cheung Chau that required a long a ferry ride across the South China Sea. Island flat (top left), ferry ride (top right), fishing boats (below). Photos by Noël-Marie Fletcher.

torch, as the Brits called it) with me in my purse. After passing through the narrow village streets, I had to climb a winding path lined with dense bushes and trees. I heard many stories about cobras living on the island. Fortunately, I never met any.

    I had many magical moonlit evenings there climbing up the steep path to my apartment to the distant sound of Chinese operas being performed. I heard the traditional instruments and songs of the actors taking place in the village below. I felt I was in another century.

    Mornings, however, were another matter. I prefer wearing shoes with heels rather than flats. And when a person is always running late for work, like I was, I frequently sprinted down the hill in high heels on my tiptoes. I had to walk on my toes due to my shoes and the steep incline. Avoiding

My flat in Hong Kong had souvenirs from my trips into China. Photo by Noël-Marie Fletcher.

pedestrians was no easy matter. I often got painful shin splints, particularly from hitting the soles of my shoes on cement pavement in the village.

One day was especially hard. A dozen large pigs, stuffed in cone-shaped bamboo cages—all the while squealing death-curdling cries and shooting excrement all over the pavement—were being taken to a boat and off to market. I had never heard anything so terrible in my life. The smell of the pig dung dripping all over the path was overpowering. I dodged among the pig parcels and tried not to step or slip on the residue. The boat journey to Hong Kong took about an hour. If my timing was bad and I missed the ferry, it would throw off my whole day. I couldn't get out of there fast enough to board that boat. It was difficult to shake that experience from my mind. For at least a month, I couldn't bring myself to eat any pork, a mainstay in Chinese cuisine.

I really appreciated my trip to Hangzhou, a beautiful ancient city located along the Yangtze River Delta. I had a taxi from the hotel waiting to meet me at the train station. Many times, I'd make such arrangements prior to my arrival. I'd arrive from a train or airplane among the other passengers and keep my eyes out for someone holding a sign scrawled with my name, which was often misspelled. Frequently people who don't know me mistake my name (Noël) for a man's name if I don't use my full name Noël-Marie. This also happened in China. It was common for me to see signs meant for me with the name "Mr. Fletcher," "Mr. Sletcher" or other mistakes. The person waiting was usually surprised at my approach when I identified myself as the person because a man was expected. After an initial shock, the driver showed me to a waiting car that conveyed me to a hotel. Everyone I met at the hotel and during my subsequent interviews was extremely friendly and helpful.

Because Hangzhou was so famous for its silk production, its light industry at that time was centered on textile manufacturing that contained silk. Some goods were 100 percent silk, such as see-through, lightweight long underwear. Others were traditional robes with colorful embroidered patterns of butterflies, dragons, Chinese characters in symbols for long life, and other imagery. To sidestep U.S. textile quotas, Chinese manufacturers combined silk with other types of fiber to create textile combinations that could be sold without quotas to Americans. Back then, China's 750 silk

Views of a Guangzhou neighborhood (above) and factory (below) taken from my hotel window. Photos by Noël-Marie Fletcher.

factories provided the world's market with 60 percent of its silk. In between my journalism duties, I visited Hangzhou's West Lake with its low rambling green hills, calm waters and serene pagodas. Like numerous others before me throughout the ages, I thought Hangzhou was a fabulous destination.

From Hangzhou I took a train to Nanjing (Nanking). In general, I like traveling along railways if I'm not driving a car because it enables me to view landscapes and communities I may not otherwise see if I jet between cities in an airplane. My train travel, for the most part, was uneventful although I usually spent several hours getting from one destination to another. Once I nearly froze during a winter trip. There was no heat on the train. My feet went completely numb. I tried to stamp and shake them to improve my circulation. It was a miserable trip for everyone due to the bitter cold in northern China. Hot water for tea was available but not much else.

A garment factory. Photo by Noël-Marie Fletcher.

Snacks and other refreshments could be purchased at railway platforms once a train stopped. Food hawkers, toting their wares, paraded next to railcar windows. Passengers opened their windows to make purchases, and food and drinks were shoved into the openings.

I was always wary of eating street food due to risks of illness and parasites. Many foreign journalists I knew who lived in Asia had become very sick from maladies such as severe stomach problems, parasites, and hepatitis. I had heard of an American journalist who couldn't resist buying American fast-food chicken in Bangkok. He was said to have caught hepatitis and been so severely ill that his former weekend pastime of imbibing liquor and getting drunk was over. Stories went around about people vomiting worms if they had a certain parasite. I never discovered if this was a myth or not, but several British and American journalists I knew assured me it was true.

In Beijing, I knew one traveling American journalist who wished to use my kitchen to boil his stocks to kill his foot fungus. (I turned him down.) While on assignment in Tibet, he bought a pair of socks since it was very cold. However, there was some type of virulent fungus living in the cloth fibers, and his feet became infected with a nasty fungus after he wore the socks.

A food hawker sells his goods from his bicycle in Dalian, China. Photo by Noël-Marie Fletcher.

Before I moved to Asia, I had been inoculated with the recommended injections to prevent disease. However, I knew nothing about Japanese encephalitis until I moved to Beijing. I first heard about it when an American college student staying at a dormitory in China died from a brain fever resulting from Japanese encephalitis, transmitted via mosquitos. I had been traveling extensively throughout China unprotected. Thankfully, I always brought mosquito repellent along with plentiful anti-diarrhea medication in my purse during my trips. I hadn't been offered the Japanese encephalitis vaccination in the States since it was unapproved there. American diplomats in Beijing could get inoculated there, but not me since I was not employed by the U.S. government.

Throughout my time in Asia, I found the U.S. Embassy and its consulates constantly lacking in services to Americans to such an extent that I tried to avoid even going there. I received the Japanese encephalitis vaccination, done in a series of three shots, from the Japanese embassy. I also once sought treatment in Beijing from a wonderful doctor at the Australian Embassy. It's amazing that no American doctors would provide me with medical care (since I wasn't a diplomat), but physicians from other countries could and did.

My time in the ancient former capital city of Nanjing was wonderful. I enjoyed meeting the people I interviewed, liked my translating entourage, and thought the city was spectacular. Next to the birthplace of Confucius in Suzhou (Soochow), Nanjing became one of my favorite places in

I'm standing in Nanjing in front of the mausoleum to Sun Yat-sen.

China. There were many interesting historical sites to visit during my free time, which was limited.

The place I looked forward to visiting the most was the hall of the Sun Yat-sen Mausoleum, located on the slope of the Purple Mountain. I have a photo taken of me posing at the main blue-tiled gate, after I made the long ascent up the stairs. At that time, my knowledge of Chinese history was not as extensive as it became after I lived in Beijing. Nevertheless I held Sun Yat-sen (1866–1925), the founding father of modern China, in high regard. I had read about his life, many personal tragedies and untimely death. So I looked forward to visiting the tomb of this great man.

From Nanjing, I traveled west by train for nearly four hours to Shanghai, which became a favorite and frequent destination. My guide was a 20-something-year-old Shanghainese businessman, who accompanied me. I usually traveled by myself. He spoke no English, and I spoke no Chinese. That didn't stop us from having a great time together. Thanks to my trusty pinyin phrase book, I chattered with him nonstop. We both laughed through our broken conversation. I'd look

A Chinese businessman and I exchange a traditional gam-bei toast with red Chinese wine.

up the words I wanted to say and try to pronounce them. He corrected me if he understood them. If he didn't have a clue what I was trying to say, I'd point out the word in Chinese characters, and we'd have a good laugh over it. At first, he was quite nervous around me but soon he became comfortable enough to share some personal information about himself. I told him about myself as well. During the following days in Shanghai, he was among my entourage, and we continued to get along famously. He was such a nice man and very chivalrous in his conduct towards me. We spoke through an interpreter in Shanghai, where I learned more about him. He was very short, while I was very tall and thin.

Once I was complimented during a banquet in Shanghai after my interview at a company. (The dinner banquet was a routine conclusion to an afternoon interview.) One of my hosts told me I had the figure of a bean sprout. My mouth agape, I was so shocked at this description I didn't know what to say. I'm certain the look on my face conveyed my feelings. My hosts quickly assuaged my fears by explaining it was a compliment over my slender figure. They explained that classical Chinese beauties had willowy figures like mine. We all laughed at the table and enjoyed a *gam-bei* toast with Chinese firewater alcohol. I enjoyed my cigarettes and white lightning liquor toasts at diner, having no trouble keeping up with the guys, who looked upon me with a mixture of admiration and awe.

Chapter 3: Shanghai

My first sights of Shanghai occurred from the backseat of a taxi as I was conveyed from the train station to the Peace Hotel, located alongside the Bund, a winding paved promenade next to the murky waters of the celebrated Huangpu River. Long leafy tree branches swayed gracefully over broad streets bordered by once sumptuous colonial estates with time-stained facades. I liked the city instantaneously, frequently thinking how much I'd like to live there. Bicycles clogged the streets, making travel slow and tedious. The taxi driver constantly honked his horn as I eagerly looked out the windows.

With great care, I had selected an art deco gem called the Peace Hotel, which has two buildings. I made sure I would stay in the building that once was the old Cathay Hotel. In a room there in 1930, Noël Coward, among my top five favorite writers, penned a play called "Private Lives." The Peace Hotel, with its distinctive pyramid roof, became the only place I'd stay during my many trips to Shanghai. Known for its illustrious former grandeur, the hotel was once occupied by the Japanese Army in World War II.

Shanghai was THE place I'd always wanted to see. I'd done a fair amount of reading about the decadent days of Shanghai before the 1949 Chinese Communist takeover.

As a former crime reporter, I was intrigued by the long-gone infamous Chinese gangsters and European characters whose legends live on in the wicked city's lore. I'd also spent hours over many meals in Hong Kong with a South Korean journalist I'll call Martin, who was born and raised in Shanghai. Much older than myself, Martin was a distinguished and handsome career journalist who worked at the same newspaper I did. Martin was very personable, and we got along famously, sharing similar outlooks on life and common interests. Tall by Asian standards, he was particular about his appearance. He wore his thick black hair combed back and was always well dressed. He spoke French, Cantonese, Korean, Mandarin and English with ease.

He went out of his way to help save me from making mistakes as I covered the High Court (Supreme Court) under the British legal system. I was covering news according to American journalism standards, which could have landed me in hot water had it

European-style buildings lined Shanghai's cityscape. The Peace Hotel has a distinctive pyramid roof (top left), which also was visible from the Huangpu River (lower left). Photos by Noël-Marie Fletcher.

not been for Martin's intervention at night in the newsroom as I wrote my stories. On most nights, Martin stopped by my desk to chat as I wrote about a criminal case.

I covered major murder trials as well as other criminal cases I found interesting. The other reporters and I had a weekly calendar list of cases each week; we'd pick some of the same ones and I also covered some by myself that took place in the courtrooms.

One case I'll never forget was a one-armed vegetable hawker accused of killing his fruit-selling wife who he believed to be cheating on him. He used the murder weapon of choice in Hong Kong—a meat cleaver. A Queen's Counsel prosecutor flew in from London to participate in the case, as did an expert in blood spattering, who reconstructed the Crown's version of the case from the droplets and sprays on objects.

In the United States, it's standard practice to interview a jury after a verdict, which is exactly what I did once in Hong Kong— glad to have beaten my colleagues from other newspapers.

When Martin heard about my scoop, he cautioned me to drop the quotes from jurors, explaining they were permanently off-limits. Heeding his words, I wrote the article as a straight hard news piece about what happened in the courtroom rather than including hallway conversations. Another

Ancient Chinese dwellings in Shanghai. Photos by Noël-Marie Fletcher.

close call I had was at the conviction of a murderer. He yelled out in Cantonese from the prisoner's dock as the verdict was rendered. I turned to a Chinese person and asked what the man screamed out. She told me. I put that in my article. However, the official language of the court was English, and the man's shouts were not translated into English before the jury. Therefore I couldn't print his reaction—even though all the Chinese people in the courtroom knew what he said. Once again, I was prevented from making a mistake.

Martin and I became good friends for the remainder of my years in Hong Kong until I moved to Beijing, and we lost touch. One of five boys, he was born in Shanghai in the French Concession before the outbreak of World War II. His father

A view of urban Hong Kong. Photo by Noël-Marie Fletcher.

was a wealthy merchant. We often met for lunch or dinner, during which he entertained me with tales about life in Hong Kong and Shanghai as well as providing me with advice about how to make my cultural transition easier.

He told me that while he was a boy in Shanghai, he and his friends would play in the fields where they came across white cloth bundles. One day, he and his friends took sticks and probed these bundles, which turned out to be the bodies of infant girls whose parents abandoned them to smother since the children weren't born boys.

Martin described how the rich Europeans in Shanghai used to carry gold bars instead of currency in their pockets. He said that the police toted huge whips to beat the beggars off people. The beggars would gather on the ground outside doorways of nice restaurants where people feasted on delicacies. The poor would clutch onto people. If you handed out money to one, then others would crowd around you to tear off your clothes or whatever they could. The police would storm up and swat the urchins like flies.

He also described the social collapse of Shanghai prior to its takeover by the Communists. His father's vast wealth amounted to worthless paper bills carted around in wheelbarrows. After the Communist takeover in 1949, Martin's two elder brothers fled to Hong Kong.

His father sold everything so that he and his parents also could take refuge in Hong Kong. On the day Martin entered

Hong Kong, he recalled that his brother awaited at the border crossing. Martin remembered his father pushing him over the border so his brother could grab him, take him to a corner and strip off his clothes to get money to bribe the border guards so the rest of his family would be allowed to come across.

I'm leaving work in the Central District of Hong Kong.

Once in Hong Kong, they were lucky enough to have a tiny two room apartment instead of sleeping in staircases, on sidewalks or in cardboard huts like most other refugees. After Martin arrived, Hong Kong experienced a drought. It was unable to meet the needs of an influx of 2 million refugees from China. Martin told me he recalled people had to drink water from toilets.

No longer able to visit his birthplace, he asked me to take a photo of the address where his family home once stood. He wasn't sure if it existed any more. It did. I found the street and number of the broken-down brick house. Martin was keen to hold the photo in his hands. He stared at the picture for a long time in silence without saying a word. Neither of us spoke about it. I knew his heart remained in Shanghai with his memories—before his family life was torn apart by war, revolution and exile. One of his brothers had been conscripted from Shanghai into the Japanese Army during World War II, while another brother had managed to join the Americans. Both survived. Because his brother was a Korean from Shanghai and forced to fight for Japan's Imperial Army, he was spared from the vicious treatment that the Chinese experienced at the hands of the Japanese military. He explained the reason was that since Korea was a colony of Japan at that time, Koreans in China were considered vassals of Japan rather than conquered peoples.

After I returned from my first trip into Shanghai, I told Martin about a negative experience I had interviewing a Chinese businessman who had been a former People's Liberation Army soldier. This man described his past with pride and had no problem relating to me his contempt for Americans. Before I left the interview, when people where shaking hands in good-byes, the man held my hand and told me: "You know Americans killed Chinese people." I asked him what he meant. He replied that during the Vietnam War, Chinese soldiers who assisted the Viet Cong and North Vietnamese Army were murdered by Americans. I was so shocked by his words and behavior that I could make no reply. I'd never heard at that time about Chinese military assistance provided to the North Vietnamese. So I quickly moved away from him and to the next person for a farewell handshake.

Martin was absolutely furious to hear about this. He shook his fist and hit the table. "Listen, the next time someone tells you something like that, don't you listen! You tell them that the Americans saved lives in China after World War II. I was a boy, and we were all starving. We'd wait for the airplanes to drop off bundles of cans. We stood in line for two hours at 5 a.m. to get a piece of bread. We lived on U.S. military sea rations for a year. You tell about that!"

I never had a reason to follow his advice in that matter, but I certainly would have if the need arose. Martin was very pro-American in his attitude and statements. When I knew him, he was divorced, alone and a Korean who had never lived in Korea—neither in what became North or South Korea. A man without a country. I've known a few stateless exiles in my life. They always pine for a world that no longer exists and one they can never return to except in their thoughts or by looking at photos from forgotten days. It is very sad.

I heard from an old British journalist about the premiere of the 1939 movie called the "Hunchback of Notre Dame" in Shanghai. All the hunchbacks from the surrounding area had been hired to parade around the entrance of the cinema as a promotional stunt. He laughingly shook his head in disbelief at the disregard for humanity and that disfigured people were used as publicity props. I had heard from many people during my time in China that former WWII American G.I.s often visited Shanghai to take a trip down memory lane. Despite the passage of time, they had no trouble finding their way around the city because the infrastructure was nearly intact even until the late 1980s. Only the street names had changed—with modern signs reflecting the new Chinese names given by the PRC to replace those dating back to Shanghai's colonial past.

After passing through the city and spending time there, I could easily understand how that could be true. The grand granite buildings and homes of the wealthy taipans remained aged while serving new purposes, such as for government buildings and businesses. I found the city to be a spectacular mix of thriving Chinese culture amid a European cityscape caught in a colonial time capsule. Both Hong Kong and Singapore had a few grand white-pillared colonial edifices scattered here and there in modern metropolitan areas. Shanghai had the opposite. Modern architectural buildings were vastly outnumbered by old fashioned, low-level, ornamented classical structures.

In Shanghai, I interviewed a manager of a prominent textile mill who was very standoffish at first. Then over a banquet

A section of Shanghai once occupied by foreign powers in colonial times. Photo by Noël-Marie Fletcher.

lunch when we found ourselves alone, he spoke to me in English. The others didn't speak English very well and didn't really understand. He told me about being in school in Shanghai during the 1930s and 1940s where he played a Hawaiian guitar, wore a lei with his friends and sang in nightclubs. He told me he was in awe of Hollywood and devoted to the films of Deanna Durbin and Bing Crosby, who both starred in musicals.

With tears in his eyes, he broke out into "Suwannee River" and some song about a kiss. His voice crackled and he sang to me, clutching his breast and waving his arms out in songs that he hadn't sung for decades, yet remembering the words. No one else knew what he was talking about. They thought he was being funny. I was so touched by his outpouring that I didn't know what to do. He told the other three people there he was singing American folk songs. I told him his voice and his memory were marvelous, and he burst into song again.

I remember being very surprised and perplexed when Chinese people shared very personal matters with me. I wondered if the reason was because I was a young American woman. At the FCC in Hong Kong, I spoke with other journalists about it to see if they had such encounters with Chinese people in Hong Kong and China. They related that it didn't happen to them. Their opinions differed as to my situation. Some journalists said I had a disarming manner which caused people to tell me things, others said I was psychic or cosmic, and still others thought it was because I was a woman.

I had similar experiences in South Korea, too, with people I met. I had only a day to travel freely around Jeju Island in South Korea after my journalism interviews. So I hired a taxi for a day to take me around. I wanted to make the most of my time. I saw women pearl divers, bought a tape of strange pop music I heard playing so that I could listen to it later, and did some sightseeing.

A manager of a Shanghai bicycle factory. It cost two month's wages to buy a bike at that time. Photos by Noël-Marie Fletcher.

At lunchtime, I invited the driver to have lunch with me. He didn't want to at first since it simply wasn't done. Eventually he gave in. Then at the end of the lunch, just before he rose to leave, he blurted out something that he'd been holding inside. With great emotion, he described being a starving kid after the Korean War and running after American tanks. He nearly cried when he told me how U.S. soldiers in the tanks threw out American chocolate candy bars to him and the other children. I didn't know what to say. I almost started crying. It was very moving. I made some comments about how glad I was that he got to have those. Then he reassumed his professional chauffeur demeanor and abruptly went back inside the car. He resumed driving without speaking of the incident again.

I had a snide Chinese interpreter once in Shanghai. Soon after our initial meeting, she inquired how I liked Shanghai. I told her I thought it was a great city with fabulous old European architecture. She replied in contempt, "That's what all foreigners say. They like the foreign buildings." I felt the verbal

Many of Shanghai's famous European-style buildings constructed prior to World War II remained largely unchanged in the 1980s. Photo by Noël-Marie Fletcher.

slap. Unabashed, I retorted that I could easily understand why. Needless to say, neither one of us had any warm fuzzy feelings for one another. She did her job, and I did mine. End of story.

I had a very strange and uncomfortable experience one day outside the Peace Hotel. I had ordered a taxi from the concierge in the lobby. Rather than grab a cab outside, I always tried to arrange for a taxi inside my hotel because I wanted to be safe during my travels alone in China. If I needed to hire a car for a day, I preferred it to picking up random cabs at different places. As a business traveler, I made sure I didn't travel on the cheap like some hippie backpackers I sometimes encountered. There would be no hostels for me.

It was at the end of the afternoon on a hot summer's day. With my news interviews concluded, I had some free time. I was looking forward to a ride through the city to visit the Wing On Department Store, which was famous. I used to shop at its counterpart in Hong Kong and wondered about the one in Shanghai. I wore a short-sleeved Chinese shirt with delicate lace and embroidery around the V-neckline. My skirt, shaped like an upturned flower, flowed past my knees. As usual, I wore strappy, heeled sandals. I liked the outfit I had put together. Both the blouse and skirt were in identical shades of a pastel cotton-candy pink. A few minutes after ordering the cab, I went outside the hotel onto the bustling street. As I held my hand over my brow, shielding my eyes from sun glare, I looked outward to the street, watching the cars, pedicabs, bicycles, and pedestrians.

From the corner of my eye I caught sight of a crippled dwarf standing closely behind me. His face was dirty, and he was clad in rumpled mismatched clothes. He looked very filthy and not all there mentally. I turned from the street to face him. I don't know why I wasn't scared in that situation—not about pickpocketing, or anything like that. I was just as curious about him as he was about me. The youth appeared to be in his late teens. He looked at me up and down with his head turned sideways. I noticed that he seemed to have a hunchback. I felt very sorry for him. Maybe he saw the look on my face. With an expression of wonder, he gently grabbed the hem of my skirt, fingering the flowing weave of the fabric.

A Shanghai businessman. The clothing worn by businessmen in Shanghai, a city with a slick reputation, was modern and Western in style compared to traditional Mao suits worn in other parts of China. Photo by Noël-Marie Fletcher.

I don't know why, but I didn't recoil. I just stood there. I could tell he was looking at me as a curiosity. Although I bought my Chinese blouse in Hong Kong, I purchased my skirt elsewhere. I doubted there were any skirts of that kind of material in China. At that time, China was relatively sheltered from foreigners, especially young women who dressed in the type of fashions I wore. My taxi driver yelled out his window at me, which caught my attention. I moved away from the dwarf and climbed into the backseat of the cab.

As I leaned over to the front seat to give the driver instructions, I lost sight of him. I reclined in my seat as the driver prepared to depart. I suddenly saw the dwarf had pressed his face and body against the glass window outside the car. I can still see his face and the palms of his hands pressed against the window. It was very unnerving. The car wasn't able to leave immediately due to the traffic and pedestrians. I wished the car could hurry up and drive away, but it didn't. The youth kept clutching to the window glass, even grabbing the rear window until the car pulled away. Before the taxi left, I looked at the young man and gave him a big wink. His initial reaction was as if he died of shock, but then he started grinning ear-to-ear at me. This episode remains one of the strangest and most unsettling of my experiences in China.

My choice of clothing resulted in another unusual reaction. I was living in Beijing at the time. I had put together an outfit of bright yellow wool pants and a perfectly matching turtleneck sweater, with a wide black belt and boots. It was a favorite outfit, serving two purposes by being a bright color and warm at the same time. I bought the sweater from a Japanese department store in Hong Kong, and the pants came from the States.

That day I strolled with a camera in hand through the great expanse of the western end

I'm wearing the yellow sweater that caused excitement among the Chinese people. I'm seated in the living room of my furnished Beijing apartment in a diplomatic compound near Tiananmen Square. I'm also wearing boots. I bought a pair of cowboy boots in the States and took them with me to Beijing. I love the way men's cowboy boots look and fit, especially those with high riding heels. These cowboy boots caused quite a stir in China when I wore them. Chinese people gawked at my boots. They had absolutely no idea what cowboy boots were. I never saw anyone else wear them in China except when I crossed paths at an airport in Beijing with two men from Montana. Clad in similar cowboy boots, they ran up and hugged me when they saw me—even though we were strangers. We had a good laugh and told each other what state we came from.

of Tiananmen Square near the Great Hall of the People. I don't recall seeing any other foreigners there, which was a popular tourist destination for Chinese from the hinterland. As I walked around minding my own business and looking at the impressive architecture around me, I noticed Chinese people stopping in

This group of young men was so much fun and great to work with in Shanghai. They facilitated my interviews and helped translate for me. I still have fond memories of our days together during my trip. I took them out to a hotel for a drink and food, which was a big treat and also probably daring to be with a young American woman.

the tracks. They laughed at me. They stared. They pointed their fingers in my direction. They stood there with their jaws dropped. I had no idea what was going on. It was happening over and over again. I continued to explore my surroundings. However, I started to wonder and become nervous.

I tried to talk to people to figure out what was going on. No one would talk to me. My Chinese wasn't very good at that time because I had only moved to Beijing a few weeks earlier. Finally, I met a young woman who blurted out that the reason for the strange reactions I received was the color of my clothes. What's the problem with yellow, I wondered? Then as I reflected, I recalled that in imperial times only the emperor was allowed to wear the color yellow. My choice of bright yellow clothing (wearing it from head to foot) apparently was a daring and unusual sight.

I found it very odd to visit shops where the locals went only to find lamp shades still being made with cloth the way they had been 40 years previous. In some stores, I found silk nightgowns in styles that Jean Harlow wore in movies. Clocks also had the lettering and numbers of the 1930s style. I went into one antique store and to my amazement the so-called antiques were things people left behind when they fled the Communists. It was spooky to see row after row of men's gold pocket watches, silver and ivory chopsticks, ornate lacquer furniture, gilt clocks, ladies earrings and necklaces of semi-precious stones and pearls. There were also at least a dozen cigarette cases with enameled images of flappers from the 1920s. The big problem was that the prices of those items were six times higher than the price of a 2,000-year-old ceramic vase. No one in their right mind would pay those prices.

I bought two articles of clothing in Shanghai from my travels there that I still have and wear today. They are favorites of mine. One was a beaver-fur felt men's fedora, and the other was a woman's calf-length black astrakhan coat. Since China had been closed to outsiders for decades, many of its industries were frozen in time. I had many occasions to marvel about this fact. The clothing articles were items popular before 1949 (not worn in the 1980s when I bought them) and fashioned from pre-Communist government patterns. It looked like the Western styles for making these items had been locked away for at least 40 years to be resurrected by Chinese companies when they were free (and largely expected to) engage in foreign trade.

These companies likely had absolutely no idea what styles were popular so they used whatever patterns they had stored away. My hat looks like it could have been worn by the debonair George Raft in one of his fabulous 1940s film noir tales.

The sales staff had a great deal of trouble telling me what the material was made of because they didn't know the English word for beaver. I knew the material was special because the hat was encased in the same locked glass shopping case as the coat and all the other fur materials. Only later did I find out what the hat material really was.

My lamb-fur coat has luxurious small black curls. It is lined in rich satin, with hidden pockets for opera gloves. It weighs a ton. I had never seen anything like it

Refreshments are sold on the street during the summer in China. Photo by Noël-Marie Fletcher.

before. The coat served me well by keeping me very warm in the icy temperatures of Beijing, where frozen winds swept from Siberia to the Chinese capital city.

At one department store, I met two lovely old Chinese gentlemen behind a counter in Shanghai. I don't recall which store it was since I always made time to browse the shops and visit scenic places when I traveled there. These old men seemed to be at least 70 years old when I met them. They were overjoyed to speak English to me and learn I was American. They explained they'd been living in the boredom of retirement when a need arose to find people who could speak English to work in the department store to sell goods to foreign tourists. It was difficult to find staff members so the store hired the two elders. One of them discussed a tragic twist of fate. He explained that he'd joined the American military forces in China in his youth to fight against the Japanese in World War II. His service placed him in Occupied Japan after the war. He had planed to emigrate to the United States where his brother lived. However, he received word that his mother in China was dying. He boarded the next boat from Japan. When he arrived in Shanghai, it had fallen to the Communists. There was nothing he could do to return to Japan or emigrate to America to join his brother. He was stuck. He bitterly regretted this misfortune.

The other man was a jazz musician before 1949. He asked

Groups of men relax in Shanghai on the Bund amid summer heat near the Huangpu River. Photo by Noël-Marie Fletcher.

me lots of questions about music, wanting to find out what was popular. He had lots of questions about various crooners. He was very disappointed to learn that the Big Band era had been eclipsed by a music he'd never heard of before called rock and roll. In fact, he was in utter disbelief and greatly saddened when I told him people really didn't listen to that kind of music anymore except special enthusiasts. He told me lots of stories about playing in bands in Shanghai as a young man in hotels and how much he loved it. When it came time for me to leave, they took turns grabbing my hand to give me lively handshakes (more like arm shakes, with my outstretched limb waving up and down due to their enthusiasm).

The music scene was an important part of Shanghai during its jazz heyday. In fact, the Peace Hotel kept a jazz band in retro attire when I stayed there. The port city had many fine examples of art deco architecture.

I made a must-see visit to the Paramount Ballroom. It was reputed to be largely preserved with its original early 1930s décor, and top floor ballroom with dancing and dining areas. I was not disappointed when I arrived one night, beckoned toward the entrance by its bright neon lights. I had high hopes as I rode up the elevator to the top floor. As I strode into the main area, I was struck by the great beauty of the walls, ceiling, fixtures and furnishings. It truly looked as great as it had been described. But it stunk. I was taken aback by a heavy, musty odor of what smelled like a mold-lined coffin. The stench was terrible. I looked around at the only people I saw. They looked like a few handfuls of Chinese thugs and cheaply dressed women slumped over a table here and there smoking cigarettes as they muttered amongst themselves. What a disappointment. I had expected some kind of happening scene. It was a beautiful dump, a regal dive bar. I turned away and left immediately.

I always felt fairly safe traveling around China by myself. The only close call I had was after a visit to what once was the Shanghai Club, one of the city's most snobbish clubs for men only during the colonial times. When I visited there one night, its baroque revival façade no longer wore a white face but was smeared in gray soot and decay. The only part of the club available to visit was a section turned into the International Seamen's Club for sailors.

The Seamen's Club in Shanghai. Photo by Noël-Marie Fletcher.

Among its most prominent attributes was its marble Long Bar (110 feet in length), which had been hacked away until only a part remained. Earlier in the day as I had traveled from Hong Kong to Shanghai, I met an American businessman during the flight. I told him I wanted to visit the Seamen's Club, which he'd never heard about. We agreed to meet there for dinner that night. I checked into my hotel, grabbed a cab later and arrived for my appointment at the club.

My mind had envisioned an enchanting opportunity to experience a once-hallowed place in Shanghai's notorious history. Instead it was a dingy hole in the wall. I don't know why I didn't realize that a place for sailors was no place for me until I got there. The crowd there was really rough. The blurred sound of different languages emanated from a bunch of hardened guys, in sweat-stained clothes, who hovered over the bar or sat lackadaisically around scattered tables. When I walked in, I noticed I was the only woman, which made me very uncomfortable when I scanned the room. It was dirty and had an ambience similar to cheap, aging diners in the desert I'd seen when driving along Route 66 through the Southwest on trips to and from California.

Thankfully, my American acquaintance arrived within minutes. We decided to sit at the famous bar to eat appetizers and drink. And, boy, did we drink. I lost track of the time after a few hours. When I glanced at my watch I noticed it was past 10 p.m. and I really needed to get going.

Shoppers examine goods in Shanghai stores. Photos by Noël-Marie Fletcher.

Since our hotels were in opposite directions, we took different cabs from those parked nearby the Bund. The streets looked empty, which I noticed and didn't like. I was nearly fluent in Mandarin at that time when I climbed into the backseat of the cab. The driver was

in his 20s and looked like a real creep. His long hair sported kinky curls from a perm that some younger Chinese men at that time wore to look cool. His attitude, mannerisms, and attire were akin to moneychangers and street hoods. I told him in Mandarin where to take me to my hotel. As he turned around to start asking me questions, he put his hands on my knees which peeped out from the dress I wore. I knew I was at risk of being raped. Chinese men never treated foreign women in such a manner.

Waterfront near the International Seamen's Club in Shanghai. Photo by Noël-Marie Fletcher.

Punishments for serious crimes were harsh, particularly in China where prisoners were paraded prior to public executions. As journalists there, we saw photos of some of these incidents after they happened. We also heard that families of the executed criminals were charged 30 fen (equal to cents) to pay for each bullet used. We also heard that medical clinics were located near execution sites because the bodies of the dead would be harvested for organs, tissue, etc. in a money-making racket.

I didn't want to show the cab driver that I was afraid. He kept smiling at me, which I could see as he started to drive away and look at me in the rearview mirror. I told him I lived in Hong Kong, which he didn't like because he thought I was a tourist. I could tell by how slow he was driving that he was figuring out what to do with me. I told him I was a journalist. I wanted to let him know that he was messing around with the wrong woman—that someone would miss me, and he could get in trouble if he did anything bad to me.

He laughed it off like he didn't believe me. That made me mad. I started to talk about my job meeting people in Shanghai, etc. He still didn't care until I dug in my purse and showed him my business card. It was two-sided, like most foreign ones, with my information in English on one side and in Chinese characters on the other side. He read for himself that I was a journalist and reconsidered whatever he'd been thinking.

Managers at a knife factory in Shanghai. Photo by Noël-Marie Fletcher.

I noticed an immediate attitude change as the car picked up speed. I was very angry. When we arrived at the hotel, I asked for a receipt for my expenses. As I watched him write Chinese characters into the empty spaces on the receipt form, I knew I would use that receipt to bust him.

The next day I was to meet with government officials from Shanghai, including a friendly interpreter I'd worked with before and with whom I was on good terms. My interpreters usually were from the local government office of Foreign Affairs. When we met, I told them what happened the night before. They were completely shocked. They thought his behavior was just as outrageous as I did. I gave them the receipt. I couldn't read the Chinese characters, but my interpreter read it carefully. She said it had his name and enough information for authorities to find him. I don't know what happened. I never heard about the incident again from anyone. However, I suspect he got into serious trouble based on my knowledge of how the government

The port of Shanghai. Photo by Noël-Marie Fletcher.

A Shanghai brand of beer. Photo by Noël-Marie Fletcher.

system worked.

Today, the dingy International Seamen's Club is long gone. And that portion of the Long Bar that I sat at has been incorporated into the upscale Waldorf Astoria in Shanghai.

One of the loveliest places I liked to visit in Shanghai was the old city in a classical Chinese garden, dating back to 1577, called Yuyuan. Despite it being a popular tourist attraction, the elaborate architecture and ponds made me feel like I was walking inside a Ming Dynasty scene painted in delicate brush strokes on a silk hand scroll. I've always loved Chinese architecture, so rich in symbolism and intricate geometric beauty. Chinese temples are also favorites of mine, particularly the Tiantan (the Temple of Heaven) and Summer Palace in Beijing.

Yuyuan in Shanghai (above and below). Photos by Noël-Marie Fletcher.

Instead of avoiding a tourist jaunt in Shanghai, I once took a river cruise down the Huangpu River that flows through the city and

Shanghai cruise to the Yangtze River. Photo by Noël-Marie Fletcher.

traveled along the shadowy waters to the Yangtze River Delta. Passengers were given a small white cotton neck scarf as a souvenir. I think I still have mine somewhere. I kept it since I liked the retro look of it, but have only worn it a couple of times since the size is so small it barely fits. The cruise provided an interesting look at the cityscape from the river. Water from the polluted river periodically sprayed onto me. I was careful to wipe it off.

The brown color of the water changed to yellowish when we reached the Yangtze. Once our vessel left the metropolis, the journey became more picturesque. Chinese junk fishing boats bobbed along. The bat-wing sails of the wooden junks wafted through the sky like the fluttering of Chinese paper folding fans. Sitting on my chair on the deck, I felt the warm sun as I surveyed this mighty Yangtze River of lore, the breathtaking views of the waterway and its surroundings. It became one of many times in China when I felt like I was experiencing what it must have been like over 100 years ago. During my life at times I have wondered what I would see in certain places if I had lived 100, 200 or even 300 years ago, not expecting to really have any answers. Yet, when I traveled to many places in China, I felt like time stood still—affording me windows from which

A bat-wing junk (above) on Huangpu River. Other junks on the Yangtze River (below). Photos by Noël-Marie Fletcher.

to picture ancient times.

As I traveled throughout China, I became knowledgeable about the distinctive types of food in various regions. My favorites are the food from Beijing (northern style), Sichuan (spicy), and Shanghai (seafood). In Shanghai, I always made a point of ordering crystal shrimp and prawn dishes. The city also had a great Indonesian curry restaurant I discovered and visited each time I was in Shanghai.

A layer of pollution hovers over Shanghai from this view of the Huangpu River coastline. Photo by Noël-Marie Fletcher.

I liked Chinese food so much that when I lived in Beijing I asked at a government office for assistance in finding someone to teach me how to make my favorite dishes. They located a chef at a restaurant who was willing to come to my apartment to teach me how to cook. However, he spoke no English at all. My Chinese was good, not perfect, so I agreed.

The chef was a tall, slick young guy with one of those strange curly perm hairdos. He had the swagger of Elvis and the tough attitude of Steve McQueen. We immediately got along well. We drank lots of American colas and smoked lots of cigarettes to the modern music I played from my imported CDs. I listened a lot to the Cure, Depeche Mode, and U2. I had a steady supply of colas in my kitchen. I always had several cases on hand since there was a bottling facility in Beijing. And, I smoked foreign menthol cigarettes that looked like brown mini-cigars. He found all of this very cool, jumping right in to join me as we got down to the serious business of Chinese cuisine.

First, I needed the correct tools—a wok, stove ring, lid, chopper (cleaver), ladles, long chopsticks) and main ingredients (peanut oil, soy sauce, Chinese vinegar, sesame oil, sugar, cornstarch, Shaoxing cooking sherry). We argued quite a bit about MSG. He thought it was essential, I thought not. I won. Selecting a wok was a process that involved a few trips to various stores. He examined the metal pans, holding them upside-down, pinging the sides to examine the thickness.

My coffee table in Beijing, with my cigarettes, film canisters, and a newspaper. This was a central place for entertaining my cooking teacher and friends. I designed and had the table handmade in Hong Kong. Photo by Noël-Marie Fletcher.

He insisted that the taste of the food was tied to the metal in the wok. I didn't believe him. He won. He finally settled on a wok that weighed a ton, looked like a big metal helmet, and had no handle (only a hole in a side metal spout where I found find a piece of wood to insert, which I never did). The wok was solid, prone to rust, and the ugliest wok I've ever seen either before or afterwards.

We meet weekly for a few months. Each session would be one of my favorite recipes that he showed me how to cook, such as stir-fried battered fish, kung pao shrimp, *jiaozi* (meat dumplings), sweet and sour pork, braised Chinese spinach in oyster sauce, and basi pingguo (toffee apples). He was a great cook who took pride in his work as well as traditional methods, which included presentation of food on a platter. Because many typical dishes have the head and limbs of an animal next to the body served on a plate, he tried to teach me how to fry the head of a fish with its mouth open. I couldn't handle that. The head and tail of the fish went into the trash. After each lesson, we'd down more cola with the food we'd just made, smoke more cigarettes, and plan to continue the merriment with another dish the following week.

He seemed like a great guy until he showed a very ugly racism against Africans. There were many African diplomats and their families in Beijing and other Chinese cities. I'd heard that China wanted to show itself to be a leader among Third World countries so it subsidized costs for having the African diplomatic corps there. The Africans, who mostly spoke French and fluent Chinese, appeared to be poorer than other diplomats. They sent their children to Chinese schools in contrast to the offspring of other diplomats, who attended private schools in English or their native tongues.

There was always talk about many Chinese being racist against Blacks and Africans. People told stories about how Chinese girls (particularly young high school and college students) would form relationships with Africans to get ahead in life. If the girls became pregnant with children from African fathers, they killed their babies by flushing them down toilets.

I witnessed ugly discrimination against Africans when I went shopping for weekly cooking ingredients with the chef. If he saw any Africans buying groceries, he yelled slurs in their direction. They showed no reaction at all, but clearly heard what he said in Chinese. The first time he did this with me, I grabbed his arm and told him not to say those things. He didn't listen at all. He continued to make derogatory racist remarks loud enough for most people in the store to hear.

I think his discriminatory attitude was prevalent among many Chinese. When I saw African men, women and children going about their ordinary lives in Beijing (not partaking in official business), I do not recall ever seeing them with Chinese companions.

Before concluding this section on Shanghai, I think it's important to discuss the Shanghainese people. I learned that Chinese people made distinctions about the types of people living within their country based on so-called attributes of different regional areas. The people from Shanghai had a reputation for being sneaky, sophisticated big-city crooks. I got along well with the Shanghainese people I've known. While there, I was impressed with one young guy about my age who was a business acquaintance. He was a hard worker who wanted to get ahead in life. I had no problem with that. Motivation to work could be a real obstacle for some Chinese who were so accustomed to the Chinese Communist emphasis on workers' equality. Take, for instance, the *xiu-xi* (pronounced shoe-she). All workers were entitled to take an afternoon nap. Many foreign companies had to provide cots for offices and factories for sleep time. If I went to businesses or restaurants shortly after 1 p.m. and had trouble finding people, eventually someone would come along to explain they were doing the *xiu-xi* thing. This napping custom is still popular.

As I became more familiar with Chinese people, I learned there were distinctions between races such as the Hakka, Han, and Manchu peoples. After I first moved to Beijing, I briefly resumed formal Mandarin lessons. The instructor was a diminutive Chinese woman in her mid-20s with a pale complexion and hair pulled tightly away from her uptight face.

After the first lesson, I found she was humorless. She brought two melon-green colored pinyin textbooks with some odd phrases. It listed a popular greeting as, "How's your health?"

However, I never heard anyone at all inquire about a person's health as a greeting. One weekly lesson was about medical-related dialog. I learned the words for snot as well as bathroom terms—not much use, I found. The instructor loved to hear herself pronounce words in an exaggerated tone—*streeetching* out each syllable. Her face was always plastered with heavy makeup. She acted very conceited. I could never figure out why until a chance encounter. A Chinese interpreter who had worked for me came over to visit my apartment one day while the Mandarin instructor was leaving. The two women exchanged icily polite greetings, saying a few things to each other.

When the instructor left, my interpreter told me: "She's a Man!"

I thought I hadn't heard correctly since the instructor clearly appeared to be a woman. "No, she's a Man!" came the reply. I still didn't understand. We spoke at length until I finally understood. My visitor, who strongly disapproved, was a Han Chinese in contrast to the instructor who was a Manchu. From northern Manchuria, the Manchus had been the ruling class in the last dynasty, called the Qing. They were ousted along with the Emperor Puyi, the last emperor. I figured that since the teacher was a Manchu that could explain her superior attitude. I disliked her and quit the lessons. I kept the books as I embarked on learning Chinese by myself through experience rather than in a semi-academic atmosphere.

I had learned the word for Sunday as *xing-shi tian*, translated as "week" and then "heaven" (*tian*) to designate the day. A mandatory maid was assigned by the government to my apartment, located in a diplomatic compound, in Beijing. The maid acted as though she spoke no English, but there were times over the course of two years when it was clear she understood English. Despite her feigned ignorance and refusal to speak English, I invited her to sit down with me and have Chinese tea every morning when she came into my apartment. I was uncomfortable having a maid and didn't treat her like a servant. I'd bring out my pinyin phrase book and dictionary. She'd put on the kettle and then we'd converse. We talked about many things. I told her about my relatives as well as anything else that came to mind.

Statue of a Chinese god in a hotel lobby. A Chinese soldier (right) studies the image, while I bow down in fun before it. I met a former Red Guard soldier in Shanghai who told me he once needed help so he went to a Chinese temple to pray. But since he was in the military, he only knelt down on one knee before a deity. He believed his prayers went unanswered due to his pride about not bowing down on both knees. He said if he ever prayed again it would be on both knees. Upper photos by Noël-Marie Fletcher.

At times, she asked questions that seemed as if she was trying to obtain information about my comings and goings. I expected this. I had nothing to hide so I answered her honestly. I came to like her a lot. I once caught her taking my shoes, discarded pantyhose, and plastic kitchen wrap out of the trash to take home. She was very embarrassed, and I felt bad for her. I acted like it was no big deal and ended up asking her if she wanted things before I discarded them. She took everything, even items that I didn't think she could use.

When we chatted, we knocked heads over the word for Sunday. She wouldn't budge, and I didn't either. I said "heaven day"—a pre-Communist term. She'd try to correct me each time to say *xing-shi ri* ("week" and then "day"). By using this term, she wanted to take any religious meaning out of the word Sunday, but I insisted on saying "heaven."

During my time there, Shanghai was the second most crowded city in the world after Mexico City, without the modern conveniences necessary for its large population. There was no sewer system. Human and chemical waste from waterfront factories clogged the vast river network. One day I was driven to a textile factory and passed black crusty rivers, with boats and people living there. Some Westerners who lived in Shanghai told me the Huangpu River, which ran through the city center, had caught fire at least twice that year. I used to pray that the wind would not blow because the horrible smell would make you sick to your stomach.

The famous commercial gateway to China is the Huangpu River. Photo by Noël-Marie Fletcher.

Chapter 4: The Cultural Revolution

A central government mandate to purge mainland China from any remaining traces of Westernism, capitalism or traditional Chinese society, the Cultural Revolution (1966–1976) was a very dark period in Chinese history. In that period, Chinese Communist revolutionary and founding father of the People's Republic of China, Chairman Mao Tse-tung, and his wife, started a campaign to rid the country of evil Western influences. Thousands of people were imprisoned and murdered for being artists, writers, having gone to college, having relatives abroad or being accused of being unpatriotic.

Before I ever traveled to China, I was familiar with the horrors of the Cultural Revolution based on my time in Hong Kong. I'd met many Chinese people whose families had fled from the Communist regime around the 1949 takeover or during the decade of the Cultural Revolution. If the latter was the case, those who suffered from the political persecution readily told anyone who'd listen about Communism's detrimental effects on China.

I'd heard and read about people being stoned to death for "offenses" such as wearing pointed Western shoes (instead of the round-toed peasant ones) or for having songbirds in traditional bamboo cages. I met a woman who worked in the legal community in Hong Kong. She told me her grandparents were slaughtered by the Communists in China.

Another young woman I knew told me about her heritage within a family of famous Chinese opera actors. Her mother was stoned to death in China. During the Cultural Revolution, she was imprisoned, faced a sham trial by community party leaders, and executed. Her crime was her profession. My friend was very bitter. She told

The gold star and red flag of the People's Republic of China in Beijing. Photo by Noël-Marie Fletcher.

me China had lost its much of its traditions due to the Cultural Revolution. There were few people on the mainland with knowledge or expertise in traditional Chinese cultural activities or foreign exposures because they had been driven off or killed. She explained that those with specialized knowledge about traditional Chinese arts, crafts, and theater tended to be overseas Chinese who lived elsewhere in Asia or in other parts of the world.

On mainland China, the Cultural Revolution was a topic few people spoke about unless they felt comfortable enough to discuss their personal lives with a foreigner. Once I had an interpreter in Southern China. She was from Hainan Island, on the southern tip of China next to the Gulf of Tonkin and Vietnam.

I knew from my time in Hong Kong that this island had been a place of exile for intellectuals and other undesirables during the Cultural Revolution. I estimated since she looked like a Han Chinese person rather than a Southerner, her life on the island likely was linked to punishment during the Cultural Revolution. I learned I was correct. Her parents had been educated in universities. They were sent to Hainan Island while the Communist party cadre members in her village took control of her and her siblings. These children were separated and sent to Communist ideology indoctrination centers led by peasant farmers and the military in other villages in the country. She told me that even though her siblings were related, they were like strangers to each other because they had not been raised together.

In Beijing, I learned some people still had patriotic Communist names—such as Red Flag—bestowed on them because they were born during the Cultural Revolution. In some cases, their names were changed to prove their patriotism. As the Cultural Revolution faded into the past, I heard that some people returned to their original names.

Wherever I traveled in China I had no problem finding abundant supplies and offerings of the Little Red Book containing writings by Chairman Mao. His likeness appeared on buttons, lapel pins, etc. The cult of Chairman Mao still reigned.

In Shanghai, I experienced people telling me about machine gun fights in the streets during the Cultural Revolution since Shanghai was the center of the Cultural Revolution. The mayor of Shanghai was hung from a light post.

Store windows in Beijing near the Forbidden City and Tiananmen Square offered consumers more modern and Western fashions, which were forbidden during the Cultural Revolution. Photos by Noël-Marie Fletcher.

People still spoke about it during my travels there although it had ended some time before. I had one woman tell me over lunch, "Do the people of your country know that we are products of the Cultural Revolution? People were killing each other in the streets with machine guns."

Another man at the table told me, "We feel cheated. I was a Red Guard. We had one group of people saying, 'We are true Communists' and another group would spring up and try to kill the other because the new group claimed to be true Communists."

I met another man in Shanghai who suffered greatly during the Cultural Revolution. He told me with tears in his eyes that his

A nursery school in Dalian, China. I heard in my travels that people needed permission from their company to marry. Many companies had living quarters for their workers and schools to educate their offspring. This school was attached to a factory. Photo by Noël-Marie Fletcher.

sister died during a purge. Since his family was unable to bury her in a coffin, Communist officials tossed her body into the Huangpu River. He cried bitterly as he told me about this. I believed his story. It was difficult for me to see a grown man weep.

I knew a woman from Beijing who was about my age. Because she had a foreign husband, she felt free to discuss the taboo subject of the Cultural Revolution. She told me about her uncle, who had a habit of whistling. Everything was fine in his life until one day he found himself banished. He never knew the reason. Decades later, he learned that his habit of whistling had landed him in trouble with the Chinese Communist Party.

I had heard tales about the Chinese during the Cultural Revolution trying to rid cities of birds. I thought it was an urban myth. But when I asked her about it she discussed this in detail. As a child, she and other children were gathered by their teachers and told to chase birds in the trees. The birds were chased from tree to tree until fatigued, rendering them easier to kill. In Confucian society, the aristocrats had raised birds. She also remembered helping to pull out trees from the city because officials disliked having such greenery around. This led to a tremendous problem with blowing sand and dust when I lived in Beijing. There were few trees and plants to hold the soil down during the windy season. I witnessed efforts by the central government to create programs to rectify the situation by encouraging tree-planting.

I heard from another woman that children were required to handle and shoot weapons during the Cultural Revolution. They were sent to camps in the countryside to receive military training. This was deemed necessary for the national defense of the motherland.

Ancient artisans decorated this traditional Chinese rooftop in Shanghai (both pages) with dragons, warriors and other motifs. The Cultural Revolution attempted to eradicate historical artifacts from an unpopular past it disliked. Photos (both pages) by Noël-Marie Fletcher.

When I went on a trip to Suzhou, I stopped at the Confucian Temple, built around 1035 A.D. It was both an impressive and imposing monument to Chinese traditions in its architecture, grounds and temple carvings. I bought some stone rubbings there featuring Chinese writings and etchings of people. The black ink on one stone rubbing showed big cracks through the carvings. When I asked about this, I was told by workers there that Red Guards came to the temple during the Cultural Revolution and tried to destroy the artistry and writings of the ancients. The sacred stonework had been left with gashes—still visible in the temple rubbing copies I have.

I found this kind of brutality to people and historical artifacts despicable. Not only was it hard to believe that such massive crowd mentality could sweep across an entire country, it was nearly inconceivable to understand the lengths people took to erase the past and fight reality.

Today, I see similarities with the terrorist extremists who destroyed cultural heritage sites in Iraq due to opposing political and religious ideologies. I am sorry to see it also in my own country, where Confederate statues and other historical

items are being removed, defaced or destroyed due to current efforts to rid the present of the past. It is disturbing to learn that in this age of greater enlightenment, higher educational knowledge and advanced science and technology that widespread movements are taking hold in the United States and elsewhere that are promulgated on blind emotional intolerance rather than sober intellectual reasoning—continuing to result in persecution, death, and destruction.

The Cultural Revolution provides an example of short-term wanton political correctness with longer-term catastrophic consequences for a nation. Fomenting an intolerant society to stamp out the past, differing views, and individuality is dangerous. Not agreeing with something that happened in history or with another person's traditions doesn't provide license to eradicate or vilify entire aspects of the past.

A poster of Chinese factory worker inside a manufacturing plant. Photo by Noël-Marie Fletcher.

Chapter 5: Doing Business in China

I had many memorable encounters and found myself in interesting places during my journalism interviews at companies in China.

I can easily say there weren't many journalists at that time journeying throughout China like me, as business travelers or as Western women. At the time, it seemed that mainland Chinese were only exposed to certain types of foreigners—fat-bellied businessmen, backpacking hippies en route to Tibet, tourists clad in bamboo peasant hats, and a few pairs of adventurous senior citizens. There certainly weren't many women my age. I had long red enameled fingernails, wore pencil-thin pants and skirts, carried a briefcase, and was often accompanied by three or four government-type men trailing behind, opening taxi doors for me.

During my journalist days of travel into the mainland, where I covered Chinese businesses for my newspaper in New York. I'm wearing a sweater I knitted after teaching myself from a book while in Hong Kong.

When people became more comfortable with me, particularly at post-interview banquets, the subject of our conversations often became personal. I learned right away that they thought I was a rare breed—an unmarried woman journalist from overseas. Therefore, they were certain I must drink beer and American cola and they served it to me at every meal. In fact, I cannot stand beer. Never drink it all if I can help it. But in China, I had to take tiny sips to avoid appearing rude. Also as a "fast" Western woman, it was assumed I smoked cigarettes, which I did.

I'm conducting an interview with a Chinese businessman.

Aside from eating and drinking some food I didn't care for at banquets, I encountered other difficulties associated with my travel. What bothered me most were my aching shoulders. I had to tote a portable typewriter in a suitcase around train stations, ferries and taxis. Many places in China had been isolated from foreign influence until only a few years before I began my travels there. Not all areas of the country (even in a city like Beijing) were open to foreigners. For my news coverage, I conducted interviews of government officials and companies seeking to attract foreign investment (joint ventures, subsidiaries, startups, franchises) or sell their goods to overseas markets, particularly in America. There was little interest in importing foreign goods into China due to various factors—primarily poverty and a lack of disposable income.

I ventured alone into large cities, ports, and special economic zones offering business incentives for overseas investors. Chances are that if China manufactured something to sell abroad, I covered it in my articles or toured sites to see how it was made. The places I conducted interviews included:
- Traditional Chinese medicine companies,
- A chopsticks factory,
- Textile mills,
- Steel mills,

Chinese businessmen I interviewed. Photos on both pages by Noël-Marie Fletcher.

- Rug weavers,
- An airplane and helicopter manufacturer,
- Carmakers,
- Leather factories,
- Traditional arts and craft companies,
- Bicycle factories,
- Knife makers,
- Beer and liquor companies,
- A baby food factory,
- Fast-food operations,
- Petroleum exporters,
- Canned fruit factories.

I started traveling to China in 1986—only two years after the central government opened 14 coastal cities to foreign investment. And I traveled to many of those cities, including Guangzhou, Shanghai, Dalian, and Tianjin as well as to the Shenzhen Special Economic Zone. I visited some of these cities on multiple occasions. In addition, I journeyed to other key business centers in the cities of Shijiazhuang in Hebei province (165 miles outside of Beijing), Chengdu in Sichuan province (the last mainland airline stop for hippie travelers off to Tibet), and Changsha in Hunan province, where the train station was enormous to match the stature of Chairman Mao since he was born in that region.

I quickly learned there were many cultural intricacies involved in doing business and even being a journalist in China. I found that protocols existed for politeness, seating arrangements, and toasting during mealtimes. I needed to learn as best as I could how to behave appropriately in a very different environment to avoid unintended consequences.

One of the most important notions I had to learn, particularly as a news reporter, involved an elaborate concept called "face." This practice initially puzzled me until I became more familiar with the culture through my interactions with people. Basically, face is a public perception of an individual similar to a type of honor or personal recognition. One can give someone face or make them lose face. Likewise, people can give each other face. Also, if someone admits something negative (whether that person is the cause of it or not), it can mean losing face. I had to consider the

face of people I interviewed, particularly if I was probing a controversial topic or one that could be perceived as negative or unflattering.

A good illustration of how this came into play during my work as a reporter involved an interview with two very nice managers at a

petroleum company. One manager was involved in the business, while his counterpart saw to the Communist side of things. (This twinning in interviews was the norm.) I really got along well with these managers. Sometimes that happened, sometimes not. Sometimes the people I interviewed hated my guts, particularly a couple of hardcore Chinese Communist old men. Sometimes I disliked them as well.

Chinese businessmen in southern China. Photos by Noël-Marie Fletcher.

Anyway, I really enjoyed talking to the petroleum company managers. I was asking questions about annual production, sales, the price of crude, etc. I dutifully wrote their answers. During interviews, I typically scan through my notes to review answers, while also highlighting passages and topics for follow-up questions.

I had been covering the oil and gas industry in Asia for over a year by the time I interviewed these people. I knew the market was in bad shape, and China was no exception. Yet, as I reviewed my notes, I noticed that the numbers they gave me were changing. Nothing added up. Each answer differed from the next, not to mention the rosy picture they painted of hefty profits and sales of their crude oil. I thought they lied because they lacked experience with news reporters, particularly American ones, and faced pressure to attract foreign currency.

I shut my notebook. Turning to the men, I had my translator carefully repeat my words. I told them I had a responsibility to my American readers to tell the truth in my news reports. Aware that this situation posed a risk for them to lose face, I said they hadn't told me truthful answers to my questions. I explained that their numbers made no sense and neither did their portrayal of the business climate in China. Furthermore, I said that if U.S. businessmen had just done to me what they did, I'd leave without writing anything. I had thought of walking out, but decided against it. However, since I liked them, I'd give them another chance to tell me the truth.

I spoke sincerely. Although I accused them of lying and risked them losing face, I gave them another chance to save face. There were no hard feelings on either side. We smiled and continued the interview without any awkwardness—with the right facts and numbers.

Sometimes in their eagerness to attract foreign investment or win favor, Chinese businessmen would attempt to pull a fast one on me to gain publicity. Two instances stand out in my mind. The first was in Shijiazhuang, a short train ride away from Beijing. I had a couple of interviews lined up for my visit. One was to a leather factory that made wallets, belts, purses and other consumer items. The people couldn't have been more hospitable. They showed me all around—even to areas that I'd rather not have visited. When I thought of leather, I thought of a supple material ready to be fashioned into something. I had not expected to be taken around the entire site, including where the swollen skin had been removed from carcasses for processing. I almost lost my appetite there. It smelled horrible, just like dead animals and excrement, and I couldn't wait to move on. I had to walk around the wet ground that had been washed down from animal waste. I saw the fleshy side of skins hanging as they moved down a conveyor belt to another location for fur removal. There were vats with strong chemical odors, places for dyes, and manufacturing workshops.

This Chinese factory manager (above) was among the few women I met who held such a high position. Below are foodstuff businessmen I interviewed. Photos by Noël-Marie Fletcher.

At the conclusion, I was off to a clothing export company. This time things would not go so well. The people I met didn't actually make anything. Instead they were about a dozen fast-talking middle-aged men and women dressed

A girl, who looks like a child laborer, in a Chinese textile factory (above). A fabric cutter (middle). Photos by Noël-Marie Fletcher.

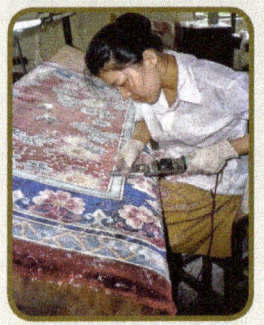

A woman trims a rug at a factory. Photo by Noël-Marie Fletcher.

in a mod version of Chinese fashion. They directed me into a showroom that looked like a part of my grandmother's living room—a cold lifeless place no one was allowed to enter into unless invited as visitors. I didn't like them. They acted phony. I took a seat and began to ask questions. They took turns explaining how beneficial it would be for American companies to import their clothing items. I wasn't sure if or how I would write up anything from that interview.

After the discussion ended, they gave me a tour of the room, showing me samples of the items they were selling. I didn't see anything spectacular there. The clothing styles looked like nothing anyone in the States would be interested in wearing since there were so outdated. When we walked over to an open shelf in the corner of the room, a woman pointed out some fur pelts. She explained that these items and others like it were also on offer. Thankfully, I didn't touch the pelts. But I took a step closer for further inspection. None of the pelts had similar fur in thickness or color. As a youngster, I'd seen rabbit pelts in stacks at trading posts in the Southwest. There were variations among the rabbit skins in colors and sizes, but they generally all conformed with one another. I'd also seen different types of fur in women's clothing. Nothing matched these.

"What kind of fur is that?" I asked.

"Dog," she replied.

I just about fell over; I couldn't believe my ears. My expression—a combination of disbelief, shock and horror—was worth a thousand words. I shook my head.

"No one in America wants to wear dog fur," I remarked. She became very offended. She took the pelts off the shelf and spread them on a table for a sales pitch. That was the last thing I wanted to see. I told her again that people didn't wear dog fur. I closed my notebook. It was like a standoff at the O.K. Corral. I told her I wouldn't be writing about that. It caused a big stink. Her colleagues got mad at me. I got mad at them. The interview ended. It seemed like the talk about clothing made from textiles was a lure to bring me into their showroom to talk. However, what they really wanted to sell was dog fur.

The second instance of tricky business involved replacing, without my knowledge, one company I had arranged to meet for another. All parties involved were in on this scheme—except me.

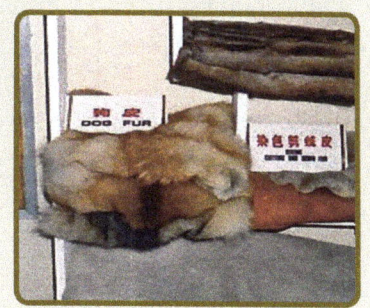

Dog fur showed to me as available for export. Photo by Noël-Marie Fletcher.

Starting the day in Shanghai, I had arrived from a hellish flight from Beijing to Chengdu in Sichuan (Szechuan) province. There was a long delay in my connecting flight. In Beijing, I had waited over three hours to board my flight, which was detained due to bad weather. There was nothing like fast-food or easy snacks to grab at the Beijing airport. So I starved there for hours in utter boredom. With nothing to do but chain-smoke, I paced around the waiting area with earphones under my hair as I listened to my imported British pop and American rock.

I traveled with a portable radio cassette player in those days. I didn't listen to local radio stations in towns I visited because they had only Chinese music. Once I moved to Beijing, I often

A showroom in a textile factory. Photo by Noël-Marie Fletcher.

listed to Peking opera on the radio in my apartment and in the car while driving around town. Unlike many foreigners, who despise the falsetto vocals and shrill instruments and gongs of Chinese opera, I actually enjoyed listening to much of it. I also found I could understand more opera as my Mandarin became better. In Shanghai and Beijing, I attended some Chinese opera performances. I loved the costumes and stage design as well.

When it came time to depart Beijing, I felt more than ready to visit Chengdu. My enthusiasm was short-lived as I climbed up the metal portable stairs to the airplane. I paused to stare with apprehension at the windows and the body of the aircraft. I'd never seen anything like that plane before. It reminded me of something out of a 1930s Tarzan movie with Johnny Weissmuller.

I later learned that it was a Soviet-made Illyshin passenger plane based on a 1950 model. The interior looked every bit as if from that age—from the torn carpet and broken seats leaning too far forward or backward to the shredded dingy curtain separating the first-class section. As I walked to my designated seat near the window, I saw a small refrigerator strapped to the floor in the corner with a cloth belt that looked

Businessmen place their business cards in front of them during my interviews. Photos by Noël-Marie Fletcher.

more like an ancient fire hose—like the kind you see in glass cases inside old buildings. I couldn't believe my eyes. I wondered if the aircraft was even safe for travel. I had no idea what kind of aircraft it was other than decrepit. The only other foreigners on the flight were a TV camera crew of about five Frenchmen who sat in first class. Chinese people packed into the seats in the remainder of the cabin. The air journey also was nothing like I'd ever experienced before or (thankfully) afterwards.

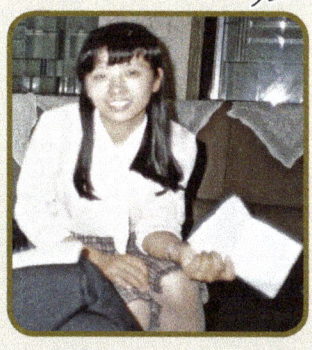

A translator I worked with in China. Photo by Noël-Marie Fletcher.

As the plane rose in the air, I expected it to keep ascending higher and higher but it didn't. Instead it maintained a lower altitude—with much turbulence—than I'd ever flown in before. The twin engines on the plane made a noise just like I thought I'd heard from the Tarzan movies.

I was very scared. I tried to calm my nerves by taking out a portion of a summer sweater I was knitting for myself. In Hong Kong, knitting was extremely popular among Chinese women. A couple of the Cantonese newspaper reporters I worked with at the Supreme Court in Hong Kong took their knitting with them to work. During jury deliberations, they pulled out their knitting needles and yarn to chatter among themselves and knit. I decided I wanted to knit. I had liked to embroider as a young teen so I eagerly taught myself how to knit. I went to a Hong Kong bookstore where I bought a book from the U.K. with illustrations of knitting needle positions and yarn patterns. I eventually became quite proficient.

On that flight, my knitting suffered. I was so nervous that my hands perspired terribly, causing the yarn to stretch thin. My stitches were too tight since I kept bouncing up and down as the plane shuddered in the sky from the turbulence. Later I had to undo everything I'd knitted from that plane trip since the weave looked like it was a patch that had shrunk in the laundry. Once the airplane landed, I thought I'd kiss the ground and my troubles were at a end. But more thrills awaited.

I disembarked down the portable metal stairs to find myself standing in the middle of the tarmac instead of next to an airport. I could see the building located a distance away. Looking around, I saw our luggage being removed from the airplane. Suitcases were placed on the tarmac right next to the airplane.

Two businessmen (above and below) I interviewed during the summer. Photos by Noël-Marie Fletcher.

Yet again, I could scarcely believe what was unfolding. A dozen or so men pushing wheelbarrows raced towards the suitcases. I couldn't believe how fast they came rushing towards us, with their shoulders hunched down, veering the unwieldy one-wheeled carts with precision. Apparently, the standing practice was to pay the men to place your luggage in a wheelbarrow for them to carry away, which is I what I did. Then I joined the other passengers for a long walk to the front of the airport building. We had to wait outside the building next to the street and taxi area.

When we arrived in Chengdu, I was so late that my pre-arranged transportation was long gone. I had to fend for myself. It was nearly dusk on a warm summer day as I stood leaning against a streetlight waiting for a cab to arrive outside the airport. Smoking another cigarette, I exhaled the smoke into the air above me and looked

upwards to the sky. I noticed a couple of dark things flying in a zigzagging pattern near the lights. I wondered what kind of night-flying strange birds they could be. Upon closer inspection, I realized they were bats.

Finally, I made it into the lobby of a hotel billed as the most ritzy Chengdu had to offer. I checked in—looking around me at some backpacker types milling around. Usually those types of travelers stayed in hostels.

Chinese manufacturers of ginseng Cola. Photos by Noël-Marie Fletcher.

Once inside my hotel room there were other firsts. Immediately upon entering the bathroom to wash, I noticed it was filthy as well as soiled. I marched back to the elevator, rode down to the lobby and got into a huge argument with the staff, who accused me of messing up the bathroom. They told me they thought I wanted them to clean up my mess even though the room wasn't scheduled for cleaning until the maid came the next day. I won that battle. After more than an hour's wait, a surly maid with a bucket slopped water throughout my room and in the bathroom all over the tiles and carpet. I was furious. This trip had become a nightmare.

I ordered room service because I didn't want to deal with going to a restaurant. I sat on the bed rummaging through my purse. I accidentally dropped my pen, which hit the floor and rolled under the bed. To my disgust and horror, I climbed off the bed, crouched to the floor and pulled back the bedspread to look underneath the bed. Directly opposite my face were piles of upturned nail clippings like melon slivers. A truly disgusting sight due to the incredible amount of these (almost like carpet dandruff) plus the fact that they were there at all.

Next I noticed whizzing noises. My room was infested with mosquitos. A rather large mosquito coil, about the size of a dinner plate, had been conveniently placed near the window. I always traveled with mosquito repellent. I lathered it everywhere on my body for the duration of my stay there.

In Guangzhou I posed with the people I met at a clothing factory. Photos below and bottom by Noël-Marie Fletcher.

The next day, I ensured I had a good breakfast at the hotel before starting my interview. The hotel was a hub for foreigners traveling to Tibet. Chengdu's location at the outskirts of the Tibetan Plateau made it a popular backpacker and hippie stopover for those en route to visit Buddhist lamas in Tibet.

Ample stories existed among journalists about trying yak butter in Tibet. Some people said it was good. Others claimed it made them ill. I had no desire to go to Tibet, which was a must-see belt notch for many journalists. I thought it was too cold for my Latin constitution, and there were many travel hardships I wished to avoid. Word had it among the journalists that there was an American manager of an American

hotel in Lhasa who was good company. It was said he was very lonely living in isolation in Tibet and always ready to meet new English-speaking friends.

In Chengdu, my interpreter was a young diminutive girl with a sullen attitude. She arrived with at least five men in our group, not counting the driver. We went to a waiting white van. According to etiquette, I was the first to enter the vehicle, which meant I had to get into the last seat in the back as the others crowded inside. We set out for my interview. I was to meet a light-industrial manufacturing company.

An eyeglass factory. Photos by Noël-Marie Fletcher.

The ride was nerve-racking. The van traveled at fast speeds along a narrow highway that left the city, heading for the foothills of a curvy mountainous area. Near head-on collisions with cars and large hauling trucks occurred every few minutes. I had to close my eyes and pray. The driver passed vehicles right and left, swerving into the opposite lane. On one side of the van was a steep cliff. The most common type of hauling truck, used everywhere in China, looked straight out of a 1940s movie. The trucks—all dull, dirty dark-green-looking ones that were open-back or had canvass covers—seemed to be made of solid steel. Our narrow white passenger van was like a flimsy tin can compared to these heavy, formidable trucks. Any type of impact could have crushed us like a piece of rice paper. I seriously thought I'd never make out of that van alive. And then we were in the boonies.

Soon after we set out, my interpreter told me that the Chengdu area was famous for its long history of military generals. Her conversation didn't last long. She began looking queasy and retching. Then the vomit came. It was her first trip in a vehicle, and she had a bout of carsickness. One of the men opened a window, thrusting her head outside so she could vomit freely, which she did frequently, as the van zipped in and out of traffic with horns blaring. Puke streaked across the exterior of the vehicle. The nightmare continued, I told myself.

An accident between a typical Chinese 1940s-style truck and a taxi. Photo by Noël-Marie Fletcher.

Finally, we arrived at our destination. A faded grayish building compound in the middle of a rural area. I wondered why an export company involved in manufacturing small consumer products would be located in such isolation.

I normally arranged my interviews well in advance with government foreign affairs personnel. Intricate planning was involved for my trips due to the journalist visa requirements, constant travel from one place to another during a trip, back-to-back interviews, etc. The majority of my trips into China were for at least a week (more like two weeks) visiting up to a dozen companies over the span of a few days. Most factories I visited were near metropolitan areas and had better links to transportation to facilitate the shipment of their goods.

My interpreter looked positively green when she alighted from the vehicle. She could hardly stand, much less translate. She had arrived at the hotel a little wisp of a girl in a prim white blouse that looked as starched and uptight as herself. No longer was she the same person. Her first car ride just about brought her to her knees. Her hair was a mess. She stunk like vomit. And her bad attitude was gone. She performed her translating duties robotically and didn't even cop an attitude for the verbal fisticuffs that ensued.

A U.S.-Sino joint venture baby food factory. Photo by Noël-Marie Fletcher.

A tall man in a Western-style business suit greeted me. He made it known that he was in charge. We introduced ourselves. I whipped out my business card, holding the corners of it with both hands in a polite gesture and tipping my head forward a little as I passed it to him.

I'd picked up polite mannerisms after watching people. Another one I customarily used is when a person pours a beverage, particularly hot tea, into your cup or glass. You bend your first two fingers (index and the one next to it) down and tap them a few times on the table toward the person doing the pouring. This custom, as explained to me, originated when an emperor or some other royal person traveled incognito during ancient times. When the emperor poured tea for his subject (who knew the royal's real identity) there was no way for the subject to bow. The only way to show reverence was to bend the two fingers of his hand as if bowing. Sometimes I notice surprise from Chinese people if I use this polite gesture in a Chinese restaurant in

A bottling factory. Photo by Noël-Marie Fletcher.

the United States.

At this factory, I was ushered into a parlor with the familiar seating arrangement of couches. I put my belongings down, pulled out my notebook and examined the English side of the man's business card. To my great surprise, I had been taken to a rabbit factory rather than an import-export light industrial company.

I turned to my interpreter and her five pals, asking why I was there. They looked sheepishly and shrugged their shoulders, saying that since I was already there I might as well interview the man. They said the import-export company couldn't find time to meet me, but this great guy seated opposite me could. I knew I had been tricked. I said I would have none of it. They needed to take me back to my hotel. They refused. I said I wasn't going to write about a rabbit fur factory. They corrected me. It was a rabbit meat facility. Even worse, I thought.

I became unglued. I told them very angrily (something I rarely did with my journalistic sources unless I didn't care if I burned bridges) that I would not write anything on this company. I had been tricked and lied to. Furthermore, I told them Americans didn't really eat rabbit meat, and I did not think there was much interest in their product. This they did not like to hear at all.

We all started yelling at each other. The sickly translator kept whipping her head from side to side like a moving tennis ball, while doing her job as we volleyed our words back and forth at each other. Their ultimatum: I had to stay, tour the facility and eat the luncheon banquet otherwise no transportation would be provided for me.

I was held hostage, so to speak. I argued that I didn't want to see the plant. I could care less what the cook was doing in the kitchen as I had no intention of making nice with them over a meal. This really was too much for them. They became enraged.

Banquets with a foreign journalist allowed them to eat all the expensive delicacies on the company's dime. They knew very well, based on my experiences, what types of foods most foreigners did not wish to eat, but that mattered little for the banquets. These gourmet occasions were much coveted and enjoyed by lots of people—even including people I never saw during my interviews. When the time came for an afternoon or evening banquet with a foreign journalist, all sorts of people dropped in. Each factory or business usually had their own kitchen facilities. Some even had daycares and employee housing.

A rock sculpture outside a Chinese factory. Photo by Noël-Marie Fletcher.

If I refused to eat at the rabbit company's banquet, it meant the people at the rabbit factory wouldn't be able to join me for a lavish meal. My gut instinct told me by their reaction that I needed to back down. I was outnumbered and completely at their disposal. None of us liked each other—meaning I had no one on my side if things got really ugly. Also I was in the middle of nowhereville in rural China.

With a grim nod, I agreed to their terms, but I would write no article. I packed up my stuff, crossed my arms in front of my chest, and proceeded to tour the facility.

It was worse than I thought. I refused to go to the slaughterhouse. The first area they took me to was a large room with lots of stainless steel everywhere—tables, implements, cabinets. The room looked like a place for autopsies in a Coroner's Office. A large conveyor belt snaked through the room with the bodies of rabbits, whole and skinned. They shared the appearance with the pinkish-purple flesh of a raw chicken wing. Their bodies swayed slightly as they dangled in the air from their ears. I nearly gagged. I turned away. I couldn't even pretend to listen to the tour guide. I'd already informed them I wouldn't be writing an article, so I wasn't taking notes or photos.

My briefcase, camera, purse, film and hotel key during a trip into China. Photo by Noël-Marie Fletcher.

Instead, I followed the entourage and tried to get out of there as quickly as possible. I asked one of the managers if the company had worked with the U.S. Food and Drug Administration to gain approval to import rabbit meat into the United States. No, they had never heard of the FDA. I shook my head. It seemed clear they had no idea what they were doing. They seemed to think they could swindle a reporter to give them free publicity to pave the way for Chinese rabbit meat to travel across the Pacific and somehow make its way onto dinner tables in American homes. They were mistaken.

After an hour of torture, I finally made it to the banquet area. The dozen people with me doubled in number as the group seated itself around two large tables.

Banquet tables were usually round; most were topped with a swiveling glass center that could revolve as people removed food from one platter and spun the glass edge so another dish would appear in front of them. In this manner, there was no passing of platters. Spinning the round glass tabletop did all the work to move platters from right to left. Banquets could be elaborate due to the number of courses served. Each dish usually would be cooked and brought out individually rather than all at once. In general, cold dishes (meat or pickled vegetables) came first. Sometimes these were followed by a soup. Rice normally was eaten in the south, while noodles could be substituted in the north. But there were exceptions.

According to protocol, I was the guest of honor and seated next to the most important person in the company. If there were other tables, they were usually occupied by people of lesser importance, such as the driver. When food was brought to the table, the host served me (usually with his own chopsticks that he was eating with) from the dish. No one else would take a bite until I ate from it first.

A white van (right) like the one I rode to the rabbit meat factory in Chengdu. Photo by Noël-Marie Fletcher.

Then everyone dived in. I learned early on to bury food I didn't want to eat in the bottom of my rice bowl. I'd scoop up a bit of rice with my chopsticks and eat it, with the undesirable bits covered up at the base of my bowl. No one was the wiser, and I ate what I wanted without offending anyone.

The rabbit banquet, however, became a different matter—more like a war zone between me and my hosts.

All was well with the first dish. A clear broth. Then came a braised green vegetable, also okay. But everything after that was made of rabbit—rabbit meatballs, stewed rabbit, crunchy fried rabbit, steamed rabbit.

The grande finale of the culinary nightmare occurred when a large oval platter appeared in the hands of the cook. My hosts smiled with anticipation and delight. I recoiled. A large splayed rabbit (slightly braised) occupied center stage on the table. Its long cooked ears had been placed next to its body, one on each side of the torso. I'd heard that cooked heads and bodies of birds and fish were displayed on plates in Chinese as symbols for good luck. I refused to eat any of it. I wouldn't take a bite. My hosts became enraged. Everyone wanted to eat, but couldn't because none passed between my lips. I protested that I once had a pet bunny (a Netherland dwarf rabbit named Claire) and would never eat rabbit. Nothing doing. No compromise.

Outraged at my rude behavior, they sat there speechless. As I said, I felt like I was being held hostage and didn't care what they thought about me. A great

A pair of vintage trucks (center) were common sights in Chengdu and throughout China. Photo by Noël-Marie Fletcher.

deal of chatter ensued among them that went untranslated. Eventually, they began to eat while ignoring me and giving me evil looks. When everyone finished eating, I stood to leave. My entourage gathered around me. My main host said little. Instead I was shown the door and almost thrown out of the building—like a bucket of dirty water heaved by a washerwoman out of a doorway onto the street.

I climbed back into the white van, which was clean again. All traces of puke had been removed. I climbed into the vehicle with the others. Our ride back lasted about an hour, the same amount of time it took to travel to the rabbit meat plant. No one spoke. I left the van without saying a word. I never saw or heard from any of them again. When I related my sad tale to my editor Phil in Hong Kong, he had kind words for "Lovey" mixed in with lots of laughter.

Another memorable trip I made was to Tianjin (Tientsin), a northern port city. Its days of colonial foreign concessions (similar to those in Shanghai) were famous. I'd read about the city's history. China's last emperor had lived in Tianjin, located less than two hours by train from Beijing. Also it became a key military outpost for the foreign powers to capture during the Boxer Rebellion, when foreign troops were sent in 1900 to China to rescue diplomats during the Battle of Peking. Unlike in Chengdu, my hosts in Tianjin were fantastic. There I met a group of savvy young men anxious to prove themselves in business. They worked with me as translators and acted as liaisons with companies to help arrange my interviews. We all got along very well and had fun at the same time.

I'll never forget having meetings in a huge old European-style home. It looked like it was built in the early 1900s and should have been located in San

In Tianjin, I conducted a series of interviews inside this former house that belonged to the infamous Chief Eunuch Li Lien Ying from the last Chinese dynasty.

Sometimes I really enjoyed working with the Chinese team who helped set up my interviews. Tianjin was one of those times. My interpreter (upper right) was great. I got along famously with some of the others who helped, particularly the men in these photos on both pages. We shared cigarettes and some good times.

Photos this page by Noël-Marie Fletcher.

Francisco's desirable Pacific Heights neighborhood. The dark wooden doorway had intricately carved flourishes and multicolored windowpanes. Although the furniture inside was new, the building's architecture appeared to be intact and the original construction. It had a beautiful vintage look. The walls had wood panels in the entryway. I wondered who had lived in such a magnificent home. My Chinese colleagues appeared disinterested in answering my questions since their focus was on business. I shifted my attention away from my surroundings to my interviews.

At the conclusion, I moved away from a large conference table where I'd been sitting and rose to explore the room. Again I began questioning the young guys, whose mood had lightened up since their work was done. Initially they had difficulty finding the correct English words to describe an important person from the Qing Dynasty who had once lived there in splendor. I finally understood. The house had been the home of a wealthy eunuch. I pressed them for more information, but they had a poor view of the pre-Communist imperial regime.

Because I'd read much about the final years of the last

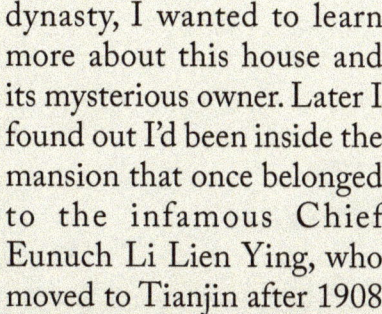

dynasty, I wanted to learn more about this house and its mysterious owner. Later I found out I'd been inside the mansion that once belonged to the infamous Chief Eunuch Li Lien Ying, who moved to Tianjin after 1908 when the Empress Dowager Tzu-hsi (Cixi) died. He lived in the house until his passing in 1911. The Chief Eunuch had been an evil presence in the Forbidden City, said to have killed opponents and aided in the murder plot that poisoned Emperor Kwang Hsu. An Australian newspaper published an obituary for the Chief Eunuch that called him "a monster of power and riches during the great Empress' lifetime, scorned and ignored from the day of her death, and left to die in solitude and disgrace though still many times a millionaire." If I'd known at that time I was in his house, I would have asked for a tour. But the men were totally uninterested in the eunuch, the house, and its historic past.

Two other events stand out in my mind as I reflect on my time in Tianjin. At the end of one afternoon, I participated in the customary banquet with my Chinese interview hosts. I remember having a good time and enjoying the company of the people I was with. Everything was good until it came time for the main course—a delicious fish on a huge platter.

Three cooking piglets hang outside a factory kitchen window in Guangzhou. Photo by Noël-Marie Fletcher.

Even though I love fish, I'd learned to be cautious of the bones, which can be difficult to locate when eating such food with chopsticks. At that dinner, I completely forgot about the possibility of bones because I was so engrossed in conversation and merriment. Until I swallowed a mouthful. I felt the sensation of a sharp needle pressed against the inside of my throat as I swallowed. I knew immediately that the pricking sensation meant a fish bone. It felt as though it was lodged at the base of my throat. I didn't want to show I was alarmed. I grabbed my rice bowl, loaded heaps of rice between my two chopsticks, and started eating as much as I could to dislodge it. It didn't seem to do a thing. I drank lots of hot Chinese tea. Still no relief. I thought perhaps it had only scratched the inside of my throat, which could explain the painful sensation.

I comforted myself with that thought, finished the banquet, and returned to my hotel. While alone there in my room, I kept thinking about how much it still felt like the fish bone was lodged inside my throat. I started to panic. All kinds of gloomy thoughts of death by fish bone in a strange land filled my head. I was freaking out. I ran over to the desk in my room that had a notebook with guest information. Some hotels had doctors listed for guests. This one had none. More freaking out. I called Room Service to explain my situation. I wondered if they knew of any type of traditional Chinese method to deal with my plight. Drink vinegar, they told me. Yuck, no way. I thought of having the enamel on my teeth stripped off by the strong dark brown Chinese vinegar they used. I didn't know what to do.

Suddenly I had an idea. Bread. My hotel was part of

an American chain, meaning it would have bread. Chinese don't normally eat Western-type bread although the Cantonese in the South have steamed sweet pork buns. I dialed Room Service again and ordered a heaping basket filled with slices of bread as well as a large pot of coffee. When it arrived, I ate bread like I've never eaten bread in my entire life. Mouthful after mouthful. I felt like one of those proverbial cows that will eat like there's no tomorrow even to their own detriment. It was an ugly experience. Yet at the end of it all, that painful pricking sensation in my throat was gone. I don't know exactly what happened. I know only that the pain left.

After that incident, I made up my mind to avoid fish at all costs in China, where river fish with lots of tiny bones were readily served up in banquets.

I'm posing for a group photo with Chinese businessmen in Tianjin.

I'm touring a machine tool factory in Tianjin. Below is a workshop in the factory, photo by Noël-Marie Fletcher.

The next day brought yet another memorable incident in Tianjin. I had downtime during the middle of the afternoon with no interviews. I relished the thought of chilling in my hotel room with my shoes off—nowhere I had to be, no one I had to see. I could write my articles to file with Phil in Hong Kong during the day instead of at night.

I've always had an interest in cinema and minored in film during college. I love foreign films and watch all kinds. When I travel or live overseas, I often attend cinemas and watch local TV shows.

That day, I set myself up comfortably in my room. The hotel was modern. I wanted for nothing. I'd met the chef in the kitchen earlier in my stay. He was a lonely American guy who showed too much interest in me. I was trying to eat by myself at a table one day, but he kept coming over, trying to chat me up. It was irritating. Wishing to avoid future similar encounters, I decided Room Service would meet my mealtime needs. My mainstay course at that hotel became spaghetti Bolognese.

I placed my order, turned on the TV with the volume down, and reclined on the plush bed while awaiting a knock on the door some minutes later. There wasn't much to see. I switched channels a few times just to learn what was on offer on local Tianjin TV. I found a cooking show. Even though I'm not much of a cook, I thought it might provide interesting viewing. My food arrived. I set up the tray, removed the metal cover of the plate and started to eat as I watched the TV screen.

An outdoor scene showing green grass appeared. The camera focused on a puppy jumping up and down, and zoomed in. I wondered why the puppy was acting frantically. Then I saw a man standing next to a large dog tied up to a tree. The dog was alive, or at least it looked that way. I frowned at the screen, trying to figure out what was going on. Then I saw the man held a meat clever, which he stuck into the side of the dog and began slicing into the rib cage.

I spit out my food as I leapt across the bed to the TV and turned it off. Words alone were insufficient to capture the range of emotion I felt—shock, disgust, disbelief and horror. I couldn't believe what I'd just seen. I felt so bad for both the puppy and the other dog. I pushed aside my spaghetti, smothered in red tomato sauce like the red blood I'd just seen on the TV screen. I could no longer eat that dish at that hotel. In stunned silence, I asked myself what I was doing in such a foreign land with a culture so different from my own.

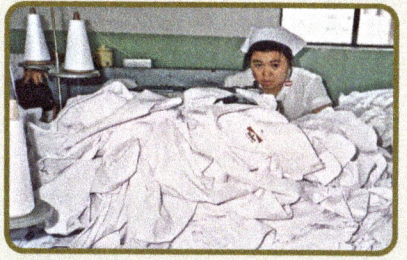

A Tianjin textile factory where workers made shirts for export. Photos by Noël-Marie Fletcher.

My journalism work took me to many different parts of China. I never realized how large and diverse the country really was until I was there. From the faraway distance of the United States, it's easy to think that China is all one country with little variation among the people, the culture, the languages spoken or even the cuisine.

The furthest corner I ventured to was the northeast port city of Dalian, once called Port Arthur. The city had a fascinating history. It was once claimed at different times by both Russia and Japan. The Yellow Sea separates the eastern coast of Dalian from North Korea.

European architecture (above and below) in Dalian. Photos by Noël-Marie Fletcher.

In terms of travel to far northeastern reaches of China, I went no farther than Dalian. Some of my journalist friends went more inland to the northern city of Harbin, some 500 miles away from Vladivostok.

Harbin was a belt notch for foreign correspondents due to its extreme cold and isolation. The city created a popular event in 1985, a year before I first ventured into China. The Harbin Ice and Snow Festival attracted lots of reporters. The festival offered breathtaking outdoor sculptures and buildings made of ice. Never fond of the cold, I declined to go with a group of reporter friends and neighbors who decided to trade boredom in Beijing for a winter adventure in Harbin. I'd heard stories about Harbin being so cold in winter that it was unwise to drink warm coffee in a hotel before venturing outdoors— your teeth could crack if you opened your mouth too quickly due to the extreme outdoor cold.

Dalian was a beautiful city with Russian architecture and some Japanese-style buildings. I marveled at the cityscape as I rode in taxis through the streets. Although it was a Chinese city, it had an exotic feel like it was a crossroad of different worlds. I noticed a dominant presence of Japanese companies and businessmen there unlike in other Chinese cities.

Japanese businessmen had a very strange relationship with

their Chinese counterparts. If there was a choice with whom to do business, a Chinese firm seemed more likely to opt for a Japanese company over an American one. After all, they

A Dalian street scene. Photo by Noël-Marie Fletcher.

shared similar characters in their language. I was told they could communicate in writing even if neither party spoke the other's language. I'd also been warned that Japanese businessmen could treat Western women reporters very badly due to sexism. I never experienced this.

When I met a Japanese banker in Beijing for an interview, I braced myself for an unpleasant encounter. However, the banker had been in New York for many years. Very Americanized, he treated me warmly and with respect. He asked me for my thoughts about the Chinese businessmen, which I shared. He told me he was having difficulty understanding them at times. This surprised me very much since I thought the two cultures shared many similarities.

"Here's the difference," he explained. "An American businessman wants to see a change in a company within five years and a Japanese businessman in his lifetime. But the Chinese," he shrugged his shoulders, "they can keep doing something forever without ever seeing it come to pass. Look at the Great Wall. They kept building it for years and years without ever seeing it finished within a person's lifetime." He added something like, "So how do you deal with people like that?"

The Chinese had a real problem with the Japanese due to World War II. Despite being able to work together, bitterness remained about the inhumane treatment meted out to the Chinese by the invading Japanese military. And the Japanese didn't really want to hear about it.

I had a strange experience in Shanghai once demonstrating the bad blood between both sides that still existed after the war. I was waiting for a cab outside a hotel. A Japanese man in a business suit exited the taxi, and I jumped into the backseat. I leaned forward to speak to the driver, but he was so angry that he kept hitting the steering wheel with his hand. Punching it. I didn't know what was wrong so I asked him. Shaken, he explained in a combination of English and Mandarin that he had just been insulted by the Japanese man, who had addressed him with a Chinese term used by the imperial Japanese military in World War II. The cab driver said that expression hadn't been used since those days. I don't know what transpired between both men. But it was very clear that the derogatory expression deeply affected the taxi driver. He was unable to leave for a few minutes until he regained his composure. I never learned exactly what the Japanese man said.

My trip to Dalian was at the onset of the cold season. During my time in China, people ate food available in their particular area during a given season. Not much produce, meat or other food staples were transported beyond their local areas. This meant there wasn't much variety in the food available in my hotel. Meals were served at particular times. If you missed a lunch or dinner hour because your plane arrived late, there

A Chinese factory entrance. Photo by Noël-Marie Fletcher.

was nothing to do but starve until the next scheduled mealtime—which I did frequently.

I lost a lot of weight during my travels in China. I was already slender to begin with but when I returned to Hong Kong I was bony. Many hotels had no Room Service if they weren't part of a foreign chain or were located in the hinterland. My Chinese hotel in Dalian was good, except it was without snacks. I only had a thermos for hot water in my room. The lone restaurant served food only at mealtimes, nothing more. I didn't care for the local cuisine in Dalian so I made a meal every day (when not partaking in the post-interview banquets) of my favorite desert: toffee apples (*basi pingguo*). The dish was made by placing batter-dipped fresh fruit in a wok with caramelizing sugar. The desert was served piping hot with a bowl of icy water. If you used your chopsticks to pull out a piece of fruit from the plate, a long string of caramelized sugar extended like a tail until it broke off from the plate. It was said that the longer the string, the better your luck. You could burn your mouth if you didn't dunk the fruit in the cold water before eating it. When the hotel ran out of apples, they substituted oranges and bananas. I enjoyed all of it immensely.

Some journalists I knew went out of their way to eat exotic type foods in China, like snake. I was told the pieces of snake meat in the cooked dishes looked like slices from a belt. Another

I'm enjoying a Chinese meal with my editor Phil Bangsberg (lower left) after my travels to China.

My entourage (above) and I pose in Dalian above a new commercial area. Because I was freezing there in Manchuria, I covered my head with my neck scarf. A construction site behind the hill where I'm standing, photo below by Noël-Marie Fletcher.

popular item was snake-bile wine. I was told whore houses were often located next to places that sold snake bile wine, thought to be an aphrodisiac. The Chinese eat different foods, such as snake, during the winter because some food is believed to warm a person's body when the weather is cold.

Unadventurous with exotic foods, I ate something in Dalian I wished I hadn't. I shared a meal at my hotel with my young female translator and a Foreign Affairs guy. Both were about my age. They had been very helpful to me so I wanted to thank them by inviting them to dine with me on my nickel. That way they could order whatever they wished—if it was an imported food item or Chinese delicacy. We chattered away constantly. They ordered a tasty soup—a warm clear broth graced by a few emerald-green leaves. I liked the soup so much that I asked them to order another large bowl for us to share. Half-way through my first serving of the soup I noticed its tiny bits of brownish-gray meat that resembled ground beef. I hadn't paid attention to the meat before because it looked almost identical to hamburger meat. I pulled the spoon away from my mouth and thought hard.

Chinese kitchens didn't usually have meat grinders. Meat was cut, sliced or diced with knives. I'd never seen anything like ground beef in any Chinese food. I interrupted my companions, who were engrossed in conversation. I asked them what type of meat this was in the soup. They began talking in Mandarin amongst themselves, saying they were having difficulty finding the English word for it. Finally, the Foreign Affairs guy brightened up.

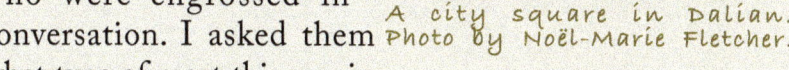

A city square in Dalian. Photo by Noël-Marie Fletcher.

"Bird pith!" he blurted out happily.

I just about fell over, pushing my bowl away. I had been chowing down on bird brains, not knowing at all what I'd been eating.

Mealtimes always provided a time for my sources and I to relax and unwind if we wanted to converse. Always interested in different cultures, I often asked questions about things that interested me personally, rather than to gather information for news articles.

Fruit is served at the end of a banquet to signal the last course. Oranges are the most common type of fruit because they resemble gold ingots and bring good fortune. If a banquet is held in a poor area, the host will provide whatever fruit is available.

One afternoon I had an interesting discussion with a business manager about peaches. The company was in a rural area lacking oranges. He pulled out a pocketknife to peel a peach for me, then he did the same for himself. He explained that this type of peach was a white one and famous in China. I'd seen peaches depicted in ceramics and paintings. I had even bought a large ginger jar decorated with peach symbols. I asked him about the significance of peaches. He proceeded to discuss how important peaches were in Chinese traditions and as a symbol of immortality.

I learned much about China and its people by asking about things I saw around me. Another symbol I learned about was the bat, which were common in Chinese furniture and wares. I was told the word for bat was "*fu*", which stood for luck and prosperity.

Chinese managers at a fruit factory. Photos by Noël-Marie Fletcher.

Another time at a banquet I was served Eight-Treasure Rice, a cold desert featuring fruit, lotus seeds and nuts. Very delicious. My hosts told me how the dish, dating back 2,000 years, got its name. I found it fascinating to learn about many aspects of China's rich culture and customs.

I visited a chopsticks factory outside of Dalian. I thought it would be great fun to take a tour and learn for myself about the ins and outs of the chopstick business.

I learned a lot in China about the various types of chopsticks that people used. I personally prefer the longer handled Chinese chopsticks over the shorter Japanese variety. I became very proficient in the use of chopsticks—learning how to pick up the smallest pea, how to use both ends (depending on what type of point was needed) to divide a piece of food, how to hold a large item from which to take many bites from (like a whole flat abalone), how to align both in a parallel position to use as a scooper, how to use one to stab a soft item (like a bun) to move from a platter to my plate. Knives were rare. Flattened short-handled ceramic spoons only came with soup if that was served. Chopsticks were the only utensil. Some had pointed tips, but many had round or blunt ends. Some were plastic, others unvarnished or lacquered wood. Although stores sold jade and metal chopsticks, these weren't common.

A chopsticks factory in Dalian. Photos by Noël-Marie Fletcher.

At my Dalian hotel, two carloads of people arrived to escort me. I don't know what type of ethnicity they belonged to; they didn't look like the Han Chinese because they were darker and taller. They seemed nervous to meet me. We got along famously before long. I liked them and their carefree attitude.

We left for the chopstick factory, located near a wooded area. I found it an amazing experience to see how little wooden chopsticks were fashioned from large panels of wood. At the same time, though, I was saddened to see the immense waste of trees. More material was thrown out than used. I thought of deforestation and how long it must have taken for those trees to grow on a mountainside only to be chopped and cannibalized for small disposable wooden slivers to be sold cheaply—then the trees and chopsticks alike would be discarded just like trash.

It was the same sort of sadness I felt when I witnessed a fallen horse carted away to be shot at a Los Angeles racetrack.

I was also greatly saddened by an unexpected turn in another interview elsewhere. I met two great Chinese businessmen when I visited their company to write about their plan to export disposable medical gloves to the United States. All of us clicked on a personal level. They demonstrated an awareness about the details involved in selling their products overseas—unlike some companies, such as the ones hawking rabbit meat and dog fur—and they were knowledgeable about challenges. I wondered why they wanted to sell plastic gloves abroad when there was such a great need in China for modern medical practices and better hygiene. One of them paused and hesitated before giving me an answer that shook me. He said the reason was that the medical gloves were made for foreigners, like Americans, because their lives were worth more than Chinese lives. "What?! That's impossible!" I replied. I didn't believe him and asked for an explanation. He hesitated again. I shut my notebook.

A chopsticks assembly line in Dalian. Photos by Noël-Marie Fletcher.

There were times in my journalism career when people spoke freely to me as a person and not as me "the reporter." If I chose to keep everything on the record and put their statements in print, they would get terribly burned. I could have ended up with quite a story, but most news stories have a shelf life, only to be replaced by your latest work or events from another day. I would gain nothing from writing it, but their words to me could destroy their lives if printed in the newspaper. These two men had limited, if any, experience being interviewed by journalists, much less from an American newspaper on Wall Street. I made it clear I wanted to understand what was meant, and their comments would be off the record.

The lives of Americans were worth more than Chinese people, I was told. Society and families invested more in the life of one American than one Chinese life. This was in terms of an investment to keep Americans healthy, feed them, educate them, etc. In contrast, the life of a single Chinese person was expendable in comparison. Also there was more potential for American society to gain something from its investment in one of its citizens. This was why the disposable gloves would not be made available in China. Instead the gloves and the better hygiene they provided would become used by a country outside of China to promote the health and welfare of its citizenry.

Dried antlers, plants, insects and lizards were among the traditional Chinese medicine meant for export to the United States. Photo by Noël-Marie Fletcher.

I told them firmly I didn't believe their assessment. I thought the life of one Chinese was just as valuable as anyone else's life.

Maybe they appreciated my sentiments. I don't know. The bottom line was that these gloves would be sold abroad and used to help a different group of people than those who made them. The hard foreign currency that China gained from the glove sales would be earmarked for some unknown use. I found this entire situation incredible.

The Communist system was meant to help the impoverished and unprotected Chinese working class. Yet it seemed to me that some things never changed. A case in point involved my visit to a traditional Chinese embroidery factory. The factory mostly was a women-only domain. The managers had friendly demeanors and a keen enthusiasm when explaining the significance of traditional Chinese symbols portrayed in their beautiful needlework. Patterns included butterflies, dragons, egrets, phoenixes, peonies, bamboo,

An embroidery factory where young girls worked before their eyesight went bad from the intricate sewing. Photos by Noël-Marie Fletcher.

and letters for long life. Decorative patterns brightened up white, green, blue, red, purple, black, and pink silk cloth. The designs adorned pillowcases, bathrobes, jackets, shoes, belts, purses, tablecloths, and wall hangings. I found everything beautiful. I enjoyed learning about the meanings behind different symbolism. The factory was very large and occupied two stories.

Up on the top floor, I was led to a large bright room filled with open windows. In it sat row after row of young girls, perhaps as many as 100. My guide ushered me through the aisles so I could seem them at work. The girls looked to be no more than 12 years old. Some seemed much younger. They sat completely absorbed—passing steel needles in and out of the fabric they stitched. With heads bent only a few inches away from fabric, they were completely absorbed bringing the images to life with their colored threads. I asked my guide about the ages of the girls.

She answered, "Oh yes, they are young. We have to have them young while their eyes are still good. After a few years at this work, their eyes won't be good enough anymore for embroidery."

This scenario looked like child exploitation to me. I saw no difference with what was taking place at that embroidery factory than the tragic stories I heard about China in the 1920s.

One hot summer I took a trip to Changsha—a dusty isolated place in the hinterland. I didn't like the area at all. It was like an outpost. There was only one large hotel where foreign business travelers stayed. The hotel food was lousy, and the waitresses were jerks. Every time I would order something, they'd give me a snarly look and reply, "*mei you*" (may yo) for "don't have." I suspected it was impossible that every dish I asked for was unavailable—none left for breakfast, lunch or dinner. I think they didn't like me for some reason and didn't want to serve me.

Hunan province is famous for its spicy food and chili. Coming from the Southwest, I adore spicy food and lots of chili. I can and do eat hot salsa and chips for breakfast. It's common where I come from to eat hot chili with every meal—from breakfast through dinner. Pizzas even come with green chili toppings. So I looked forward to trying different spicy dishes in Changsha. However, not much was on offer. I found myself eating lots and lots of spicy boiled peanuts because these were plentiful.

My time in Changsha was memorable for another reason: my hotel room became an operational base for all of my interviews for several days. I flew into Changsha in the late afternoon. My interviews were to begin the next day. I had my first rude encounter with the hotel waitresses at dinner after my arrival. I spent the remainder of the evening in my hotel room, which was decorated in worn but clean 1950s decor. It had a bed, a small round table and two chairs. I phoned reception to arrange for a wake-up call, as was my custom.

The next day, I awoke to loud knocking on my door. I looked at my watch, which showed it was still very early and not the appointed time for the wake-up call. I tried to ignore the noise but arose bleary-eyed to see what the commotion was. To my shock, a dozen Chinese people with smiling faces greeted me as I opened the door. I stood there, my hair

My camera film, portable typewriter, knitting supplies, press credentials and newspapers on a hotel desk in China during one of my trips into the mainland. Photo by Noël-Marie Fletcher.

a wreck, in my robe and nightgown. I was informed the group was my welcoming committee to their province. They were very glad to see me, very glad to talk to a reporter, very glad that American readers of my newspaper would learn about all the great business opportunities available there, genuinely very glad about everything to do with my visit.

I just about died on the spot. To say I was unprepared was an understatement. My bra and other assorted clothes were scattered all over the room. One of the group pushed open my door wider, and they all came marching in—craning their necks this way and that way to see what I had in my room. It was embarrassing. I started grabbing my undergarments and other personal items to hide near the bed.

A man started waving his arms like an orchestra conductor. I had no idea what was going on. I was horrified. Apparently, there was concern that only two chairs were in the room. Several men from the group disappeared to return with chairs under their arms. Others came in with teapots, tea cups, glasses, cola and ashtrays. I shook my head. There was absolutely nothing I could do, but go with the flow. I excused myself, grabbed some clothes and changed inside the bathroom in my room, which overflowed with people.

For nearly five days, my hotel room was like a smoky pool hall with a permanent cigarette haze. People laid around on my bed, slumped on the chairs, wandered in and out of my bathroom, strolled up and down the hallway, picked up my personal belongs (any that I didn't hide from sight) to inspect. I couldn't keep track of the people coming in and out.

Apparently, my Foreign Affairs liaison decided that all interviews would be conducted in my room. An assortment of businessmen and officials came every hour or so to await their turn to talk to me. Large groups of people kept coming in and going out. It was crazy! There was no letup. I had trouble keeping up with all the traffic, taking notes, meeting people, exchanging business cards, figuring out questions to ask, etc.

I could only question two people at a time, leaving the other 10 people in each entourage with nothing to occupy their time there during the interviews but lounge around. The only reason I could guess for their doing this was that a visit to the hotel and my room, in particular, would provide them with an opportunity to get away from their rural locale to visit the fancy hotel and examine the American girl reporter.

One of the Chinese businessmen I interviewed in my Changsha hotel room. Photo by Noël-Marie Fletcher.

Each morning as I awoke, I knew a dozen people would be waiting outside my door. I felt like I was staying in a hotel lobby rather than a room. When they left at the end of the day, my room was full of empty cans, cups, glasses, overflowing ashtrays. It was trashed. There was no maid to clean my room since the cleaning staff had already left for the day by the time my interviewing ended. I pushed all the dishes and trash in the hallway each evening for it to disappear. My bathroom had been as fully occupied the entire time as one in a busy airport. Even so, I couldn't be angry at any of them. They were all so nice. It became humorous.

Sometimes the people I interviewed went through great

A taxi at a Chinese hotel where I stayed. Photo by Noël-Marie Fletcher.

trouble and expense to be hospitable. My newspaper was prominent in the shipping world. Chinese business leaders at the port of Shanghai were well aware of this fact. They arranged for a welcome banquet for me one evening at an expensive restaurant. They were very kind. The dinner was an elaborate affair where some 50 people gathered to meet me. I sat at the table as the guest of honor. Others dined at tables designated for guests of lesser importance. There was lots of toasting to me and me toasting them. What I recall most from this event was carved watermelons. Artistic etchings with scenes from ancient China had been carved into hollowed watermelons that contained soup. I thought the soup would be cold but it was hot instead. My attention was captivated by the beauty portrayed in the carvings.

As stated earlier, when I went to China, I did so as a business traveler rather than a tourist. Few women (either foreign or Asian) were business travelers there. Business class flights were predominantly occupied by men. I didn't mind or pay attention. Instead I kept focused on the job I needed to do. One time, I needed to travel from one city to another in the south near Guangzhou. I disliked the train connections and the flights. I decided to do the unheard of by making arrangements at my hotel to hire a taxi to drive me for three hours one way to my destination. Many discussions and negotiations with my government contacts were involved. My mind was made up. That's what I wanted to do, and my newspaper had to deal with the costs. I'm sure this was viewed as very decadent behavior, but I was unmoved.

A dark sedan drove up at the appointed time. A hip-looking young Chinese driver with dark sunglasses and long hair, almost shoulder length, swaggered out of the car. He spoke no English. I made certain he knew where I wanted to go and how much I was prepared to pay. He shrugged his shoulders like it was no big deal. Then we set out.

I stand among a group of businessmen during my trip to Dalian.

I sat in the backseat, smoking cigarettes and looking at the landscape. I had a fabulous time. I saw many lovely sights—water buffalo, rice paddies, ancient city walls, intricate riverways, moon-shaped bridges, emerald-green fields. The driver indeed was a hipster. He had an assortment of American pop music, rare at that time in China, that he blared while he drove in silence. I could see him every so often studying me from the rearview mirror. I never felt intimidated or like anything bad would happen to me. I thought he acted curious about me. His favorites tunes that he played over and over were by Michael Jackson. I sat there wondering to myself what I was doing cruising through the countrysides of China listening to Michael Jackson.

This was yet another time when I marveled at my surroundings and thought I had a glimpse of what life over a hundred years ago must have looked like.

A Chinese couple at a street market. Photo by Noël-Marie Fletcher.

Part 3: China Correspondent

Chapter 6: Beijing Life

By the time I became China Correspondent in Beijing in October 1987, I had traveled extensively throughout the mainland. I thought I had a pretty good idea of what would await me living there. But life had surprises. I was unprepared for the hardship of living in such isolation, and was completely taken aback (like the rest of the world) by the Tiananmen Square uprising and subsequent military crackdown.

Once I moved to Beijing, I was told that the U.S. State Department had a 1–25 scale ranking countries from the least (1) to the most difficult (25) living conditions for diplomats. Middle Eastern countries had an average ranking of 23 in contrast to China, which had a 25 score—making it among the most difficult countries in the world for Americans to live in. Many Americans and Europeans couldn't stand the isolation, the lack of anything familiar, and the almost complete absence of any Western culture.

Most U.S. businessmen who moved to China for work purposes came alone. Their wives and children stayed behind. If some brave wives came out with their spouses, they didn't stay long. I remember once going to

My business card as China Correspondent in Beijing. The reverse side had the same information in Chinese characters, with my Chinese name, Fang Ne. It took me awhile to get used to answering to Fang Ne Xiaojie (Miss Fang Ne) rather than my given name. Photos by Noël-Marie Fletcher.

Street shops for clothing, accessories, consumer goods and food in Beijing. Photos (both pages) by Noël-Marie Fletcher.

an American joint-venture company in Beijing for an interview before Christmas. It was so cold in Beijing that day, I wore three layers of clothing during my taxi ride to the office.

Most buildings were unheated in China except for sparsely located coal-burning stoves, where people would crowd around for warmth.

If you wanted to know how cold it was in a particular Chinese city, you'd ask how many layers of clothes people there wore. Was it one, two or three layers? When you washed your hair or blew your nose in the winter, black soot appeared from the burned coal particles in the air.

As I arrived at the Beijing joint-venture office, a party was underway. A few wives were in attendance. They grabbed me and brought me to a table. Everyone was dancing and hopping around with glee. They were celebrating eating cheddar cheese and crackers. Someone had arrived from Hong Kong with a suitcase full of cheese, which was unavailable in Beijing. I was very touched that they invited me to partake in such a valuable treat. I carefully chewed my piece of cheese on a cracker—relishing every second. It was great! We were all filled with joy at this simple pleasure and sharing with one another.

I learned early on that in China there were no fundamental Judeo-Christian principles that many Americans take for granted in their dealings with others. For instance, it is generally accepted by most Americans that lying is wrong, although people do it from time to time. There is no such basic assumption in China. People lied many times if it served their purposes. If someone was caught in a lie, it was generally viewed as okay for them to tell more lies if necessary. The belief system was completely different. China's Communism was also a large contrast from American-style democracy.

I remember being asked to buy a baby at a market in Beijing. It was quite shocking. While walking around a market (the equivalent to a U.S. farmer's market) one summer weekend, I strolled past a stand where a man and woman were selling fruit. The woman motioned for me to come behind the stand, which I did. She said she wanted to show me something. She lifted a cloth covering a basket where a baby slept inside. She told me it was a boy. She wanted to sell the child

to me. I couldn't believe it. I told her I wasn't interested.

I was very shaken and left. When I described the incident to some of my journalist friends, we got to thinking there must have been something wrong with the baby. Since the child was a boy, he would have been valued—unlikely to be given up unless he had a medical condition.

Another time I found an abandoned baby girl. It was a cool autumn morning as I sauntered along the streets with

A woman and boy in Shanghai (above). A mother in Beijing walks with her baby girl on her back (below). Photos by Noël-Marie Fletcher.

my dog Paloma in Beijing's diplomatic area near my apartment. I lazily smoked cigarettes as she sniffed around on her morning bathroom rounds. That dog could never just take care of business. Instead she sniffed hither and thither for up to an hour. I let her do her thing, knowing there was no hurrying that dog.

A couple of old lady street sweepers wielding brooms made of twigs and tree branches brushed dirt down the road. They wore white cloth facemasks and round white caps, typical street-sweeper attire. Chinese neighborhoods were informally policed by nasty old ladies and men, often nicknamed "second dogs" in Mandarin as a slur since the real police were the "first" dogs. Some of them wore red armbands and sat on little wooden stools where they acted as sentries in Beijing's old *hutong* neighborhoods near the Forbidden City. These sassy elders got into everyone's business—Chinese and foreigners alike.

The street sweepers were of the same ilk. Paloma and I ignored them. They didn't do the same with us. They kept edging along the sidewalks in the same direction we walked, pretending they weren't being nosy. The U.S. Ambassador lived in one of three American diplomatic compounds. Everyone knew who lived behind the imposing iron gate, which I often passed since it was right down the street from my apartment.

That morning Paloma started pulling on her leash, as she often did when enticed by an interesting scent. She led me to a bush outside the U.S. Ambassador's gate where a bundle—

which looked like rags—had been placed on the ground. Restraining the dog, I stepped up to the bundle so I could have a look.

There was a baby Chinese girl

A street sweeper (above, left) can be seen next to me as I walk my dog Paloma through the diplomatic missions near my Beijing apartment. A soldier (top, right) stands guard outside an embassy.

dressed in pretty pink clothes. Whoever placed her there ensured that she was dressed nicely. No sound came from her. As I crouched down to pick her up, the two old lady street-sweepers swooped down and grabbed the baby. I tried to talk to them, but they yelled at me and walked quickly away with the child. I felt very sorry for both the child and her mother. It looked as if the mother had carefully dressed the baby and placed her in front of the Ambassador's residence so he would take her. These two facts indicated to me a strange kind of love that the mother had for her child, who lay abandoned in the dewy grass that chilly morning.

I wasn't alone in finding babies. I attended a lavish banquet for a few hundred people in a Beijing hotel to celebrate the arrival of an American business magnate. He had invested heavily in China and had several subsidiaries throughout the country. I was covering his visit for my newspaper. I came to the dinner to hear his speech and do some reporting. Most of my news competitors sat near his table in the front.

My apartment was located in the diplomatic compound (top, left). I'm out on a daily walk in Beijing with young Paloma. In all these photos I can be seen wearing the black Chinese men's shoes I bought after I saw an old watchman in Macau wearing this style of traditional footwear. I loved these shoes and wore them all the time.

However, I had a different approach. I chose a back table where his few Americans managers sat with a couple of their wives. We had a great time chatting about nothing in particular. I did glean some information there that helped me break some news later and beat my competition.

While exchanging views on living in China, one wife related to me how much she disliked being in the Chinese hinterland. It was awful, she said. She described constantly finding the corpses of baby girls along the roadside. The peasants in the surrounding communities wanted sons due to the one-child policy. That meant many abandoned baby girls were left to die along the road after they were born.

I really didn't know very much about Chinese Communism until I lived there and saw it in action. I once knew a newspaper journalist in Los Angeles during my early days as a reporter in Palm Springs. He pronounced over dinner one night that he was a Communist (albeit one with a trust fund). I gave it no more thought other than that he was a weirdo. Once I got to China, I witnessed a very ugly dimension of the mainland version of that form of governance. I recalled the L.A. reporter and his proclamation,. I thought to myself that he'd never have lasted in China with his elitist ways.

My first assignment in Beijing after I moved there was to attend the opening session of the National Congress of the Communist

Party of China at the Great Hall of the People. I'd been in town for a few days. The Great Hall, spread over 1.8 million square feet of floor space, was a magnificent building in which

I took this photo in 1987 while walking to join other journalists from all over the world to cover the first day of the National Congress of the Communist Party of China inside the Great Hall of the People in Beijing. Photo by Noël-Marie Fletcher.

everything was massive. The interior wall paintings depicting ancient Chinese landscapes were about the size of billboards you see along American highways. Red, the color of the Chinese flag, was the primary color inside.

I stood in a long line with journalists from all over the world as we waited our turns with our press credentials to gain admittance. We were shown to a balcony area overlooking the main auditorium where we could see the Congress in session.

Later I attended many press events at the Great Hall of the People. Each time I saw it, I was impressed. To get to the Great Hall, I had to park my car near Tiananmen Square, which had a portrait of Chairman Mao in a center position of honor on Tiananmen Tower. The portrait hung over a major archway that led to the Forbidden City. I could see hooks on the sides of the Tiananmen Tower and was told heads used to be hung from those hooks.

Journalists were required to live in housing compounds with diplomats and airline personnel in a central location, where we could all be monitored by the government. One American news organization operated from a hotel, but most others had offices and apartments among a handful of diplomatic

The interior of the Great Hall of the People before the first session began for the National Congress. I sat with newspaper and wire service reporters in a balcony (the edge is visible at the bottom image). Photos by Noël-Marie Fletcher.

compounds scattered throughout Beijing. Many times journalists lived in the same buildings where they worked. My apartment was located five miles from the Forbidden City within the Jianguomenwai Diplomatic Residence Compound. From my 11th floor window, I overlooked a major thoroughfare called the 2nd Ring Road. It intersected with the Beijing Ancient Observatory, built in 1442.

The 2nd Ring Road—which ran along the old city wall and many gates—was a key route to access the old city. I was told that my compound had been built on an undesirable piece of land used as a graveyard in ancient times. Bodies were taken from the old city past the city wall and disposed of on that land—which I heard had since become a great place to build houses for foreigners since superstitious Chinese didn't want to live there. This notion of the area being an old graveyard location was common among the foreign community where I resided. I didn't know if it was true.

During my time in Beijing, a construction project requiring

roadwork took place next to the Jianguomenwai Compound. I saw the construction and was told at that time by a resident that a human skull had been dug up during the roadwork. We figured the rumors about an ancient graveyard were true. We all wondered whether the area was haunted.

A few months into my stay at my Jianguomenwai apartment, I began to have a series of terrible nightmares. Night after night, I had great difficulty sleeping. I began to wonder if there was something supernatural about it due to the rumors of my residence being on an ancient graveyard site.

A doorway in Hong Kong with Chinese religious emblems for good luck and images of gods for protection. Photo by Noël-Marie Fletcher.

I knew from my Chinese journalist friends in Hong Kong that the local people had many beliefs about ghosts. They had paper objects (cars, money, etc.) that could be burned as offerings to give to people who had died. Marriages could be arranged between families of dead people. There was even the Hungry Ghost Festival when the dead—ghosts and dead relatives—come out to roam among the living each year and receive offerings (like rice, incense and fruit).

I decided to take measures into my own hands and fight fire with fire. Surely Chinese people would know what to do about Chinese ghosts. I flew into Hong Kong for a weekend and visited a store that sold statues of deities. To my knowledge, no such stores existed in Beijing due to Chinese Communist official views on religion and superstition.

Once on Hong Kong Island, I found a small overcrowded shop along a narrow corridor of streets far away from where the British buildings stood. The elderly man looked at me a bit odd when I entered his small shop. I spoke to him in English, explaining my situation about living in Beijing in an apartment building above an ancient graveyard. He listened carefully, nodding occasionally. He told me he knew exactly what I should do. He left for a few moments to rummage

Drivers and factory workers in Manchuria. Photo by Noël-Marie Fletcher.

around shelves with various ceramic deities. When he returned, he brought me two statues. One was a lovely white porcelain statue of the goddess Kwan Yin. The other statue was smaller, about the size of a cola can. It depicted a crazed-looking Chinese man in ancient clothing. He had wild shocks of long black hair, a wispy bird and moustache, and an ugly scowling expression on his face. He was a ghost catcher. I paid for the statues and brought them to my apartment in Beijing. I figured that perhaps a Chinese ghost would respond to these Chinese spiritual remedies. My nightmares continued for a bit. The statues didn't help, but I kept them anyway.

A peasant woman carries her load during the summer. Photo by Noël-Marie Fletcher.

I had to get a driver's license soon after I moved to Beijing. It was an ordeal. The government had stringent rules for foreigners. Before I was granted a residency visa, I had to be tested for AIDS like all other foreigners. The government viewed AIDS as a foreign disease. This was in the early days of AIDS before there was greater awareness. I remember asking to be tested for AIDS in the United States at that time. By merely asking to be tested, I was treated terribly by American medical personnel as if I were some kind of leper. They did not fully appreciate that I only needed to prove I didn't have the disease to get a Chinese visa.

A worker stands next to containers similar to those used to transport night soil via bicycles. Photo by Noël-Marie Fletcher.

To get a driver's license I had to be tested in a hospital. Chinese medical staff took my blood pressure in both arms instead of just one arm. I had to take two tests to show I wasn't colorblind. There were no driving tests to determine if I even knew how to operate a vehicle or could read road signs. Once the doctors completed my paperwork, it was submitted to a government bureau that provided me with a small blue booklet, about the size of a saltine cracker, with my photo and Chinese writing as my driver's license.

The sanitation at Chinese hospitals was problematic. All foreigners I knew brought their own sterilized, disposable hypodermic needles with them when they entered China. The needles were to be taken when visiting a Chinese doctor. I heard from some people that once the doctors used the foreign needles, they rinsed them off with water and kept them instead of throwing them in the trash.

There was only one hospital in Beijing recommended for foreigners in case of an emergency. Thankfully, I never had to go there. However, I heard descriptions from others who had been there.

An American journalist in Beijing described going to the foreigner's hospital, which was supposed to be more upscale

Typical street traffic in a Chinese neighborhood. Photos by Noël-Marie Fletcher.

than others. He laughingly described what he thought that meant. The hospital bathroom for foreigners was an open cement slot in the floor with running water underneath to carry away waste. In contrast, the bathroom for Chinese people in the same hospital had only an open slot—waste piled up to be collected later, with some used as vegetable fertilizer (called night soil).

Often I saw men laboring to pedal bicycles with large metal vats on the back that contained night soil. Because diseases can be passed from excrement onto vegetables meant for human consumption, I had a large supply of iodine I used to wash my vegetables with. Sometimes I couldn't get the iodine taste out of the food. I never ate any fresh vegetables during my time there. I cooked everything thoroughly. If I ate fruit, its skin had been peeled. I also never drank water that wasn't boiled first. If I had a cold drink, it came from a bottle or a can.

To drive a vehicle in China was a big deal—a calling, an extreme sport, a vocation, a feat for men only. Chinese drivers were an elite group of sophisticates. It took a year of study for them to get a driver's license. They not only drove vehicles, but also had to know how to clean and maintain mechanical functions. Driving was a full-time profession. Chinese drivers were a snobby group. They ran around with long feather dusters preening over their vehicles. Getting gas was serious business. Only a couple of gas stations existed in Beijing, and they didn't want foreigners there. Cars belonged to companies, which had Chinese drivers who were the ultimate vehicle bosses. They ensured tanks were refueled, tires had sufficient air, and every aspect of the car was in working order.

A Beijing cyclist drives past a street sign depicting typical Chinese vehicles, including the horse cart on opposite page. Photo by Noël-Marie Fletcher.

Foreigners drove cars around Beijing. However because I was a foreign woman driving a car, I was an oddity often stared at in amazement. Many people couldn't believe I was driving a car. They'd point at me with their mouths open.

After martial law was declared in Beijing during the aftermath of the Tiananmen Square massacre, I drove a car with another journalist to explore the city at night. When I approached roadblocks with heavy Chinese military presence, I stopped—as directed by armed soldiers—so my identification could be reviewed by them. They were so shocked to see me (a woman) driving that I never had any trouble getting okayed to proceed past checkpoints. My other male colleagues had no such luck and frequently had hostile encounters on their nightly rounds.

After the Tiananmen Square massacre, I was part of a group of American journalists who explored the city in sections as we took turns driving through checkpoints at night in Beijing. We'd return to a designated newsroom to share information with each other about what we'd seen so we could pool our resources for news reports. This was a very dangerous activity at the time. The government issued warnings that foreigners could be shot if they didn't have appropriate identification.

There weren't many foreign women living in Beijing at that time—much less zipping through traffic like I did wearing my sunglasses—with my window rolled down, radio blaring and a cigarette dangling from my fingertips. I once had a lengthy conversation with a 20-something-year-old Chinese driver who told me about how he could and did use his *Qi* (pronounced chee) energy to make his car behave in desired ways. I didn't believe him. He set out to convince me. He showed me how he pointed his hands at the steering wheel to extend the energy from his body at the car. I remained a skeptic.

My Beijing apartment was sparse and decorated with items I bought from my travels in China. Photo by Noël-Marie Fletcher.

The Chinese government assigned numbers to the vehicle license plates of foreigners. That way, anyone could recognize by a particular plate number what country the car belonged to. Journalists were no exception. We had No. 01 on our license plates. Everyone could tell where we were parked or traveling to. Most of us sped everywhere. I couldn't tell what the speed limit was so I drove as fast as I thought I could get away with. I knew one British journalist who was speeding on a long, isolated road near the airport. He wasn't wearing a seat belt when he crashed near a tree. Lucky to be alive, he warned us about driving fast and advocated wearing seat belts.

Living in the diplomatic compounds was difficult. You had no privacy. Each apartment had a government-assigned maid. Each building had a group of surly staff—who supposedly maintained the buildings—on the ground floor. They usually sat sprawled on chairs in an office with the doors wide open across from

After security cameras were installed, I took a selfie in the elevator in the Beijing compound where I lived. Photo by Noël-Marie Fletcher.

the elevators—where they could see your comings and goings. The staff members were unfriendly. They grunted at you, scowled, watched your every move, climbed into the elevators to push the buttons for your floor and looked carefully at what you had. If you carried a shopping bag, they didn't hide the fact that they tried to see what was inside. Sometimes they dragged dirty cloth mops that streaked the floor with trails of brown liquid.

After I'd lived there a year, a camera and a microphone were installed in the ceiling of each elevator. One night I'd been partying with an American journalist and his girlfriend. We were going back to his building, located in the same compound as mine, for more booze. We had all been drinking heavily, whooping it up with laughter. It was past midnight. We climbed into the elevator. Our unsteady gazes fixed upon the camera and microphones. We disliked being spied upon. He decided to see if anyone was paying attention. The unfriendly building staff had already gone for the day. So the journalist covered up the camera with his hands. We all started giggling as the elevator rose to his floor. To our great surprise—and delight—we heard a man screaming in Chinese at us from the microphone. We burst out laughing. He was furious that we had covered up the camera. We thought it was all good fun—although we knew the answer to our question about whether anyone monitored our behavior at late hours.

I knew of a foreign journalist who decided to try making prank phone calls one night. He had been bored, wanted to have some fun and had been smoking some marijuana in his apartment there, he explained. I didn't know you could smoke pot in China, but he apparently did. I failed to understand why he thought the idea of making prank phone calls would be so enjoyable. Perhaps it was because he was under the influence. Anyway, he started random dialing telephone numbers. When people answered, he asked if he could speak to Chinese leader Deng Xiaoping. His foolish prank didn't work. He thought he'd get some laughs. Instead the people tried to be helpful, explaining to him that their leader really didn't live there. He gave up after a few calls.

A common sight in Beijing. Photo by Noël-Marie Fletcher.

I used to enjoy eating lunch *jiaozi* (Chinese dumplings) in a small restaurant on the grounds of the Temple of the Sun. I bought my groceries and souvenirs at the Friendship Store, located within walking distance from my apartment.

After my first year of living in Beijing, I grew tired of the mundane daily routine. I found living in such isolation, and within the confinement of the diplomatic compounds, stifling. I answered an advertisement in a local grocery store for an English tutor. An Italian couple (a businessman and his bubbly wife) wanted their teenage son to learn to speak better English. I wanted something more to do with my time. So I became a tutor. I met the teen once or twice a week to converse with him. I didn't really have a lesson plan but would talk to him about all kinds of topics. His English was good and became even better. He was a nice kid with red hair. I met his parents and their friends in the Italian community a few times for dinner. We spoke about Italy.

In one conversation, the boy's father recalled watching bombs fall on his hometown during World War II. He described being a small child and sitting on a rooftop. He became emotional when he spoke about hearing the sounds of the American planes fly above before the bombs fell. I became uncomfortable. I didn't really know how to respond. He had no animosity for Americans, but I could see there were things he wasn't saying aloud.

Other efforts I made to stave off boredom included lots of reading. A friend in Hong Kong sent me a box of books every month. I told him to pick out whatever he thought I'd like. I really enjoyed this. I read daily every afternoon and even into the evenings. Many books

A hot summer day in China. Photo by Noël-Marie Fletcher.

I liked involved Asia and historical accounts of British colonial times in India, Malaysia, and Hong Kong.

I also drove often to places in Beijing where I could find English translations of Chinese works. I was particularly interested in the writings of modern Chinese authors. I gained an appreciation of their point of view. However, the works translated all tended to follow the Chinese Communist stereotypes—rich people were bad, the working class was great, past regimes were corrupt and abusive. I also attended Chinese movies with English subtitles shown periodically in a foreign-owned hotel. These movies, also intriguing, tended to follow the same storylines as the books. However I enjoyed immersing myself in the culture.

One of my favorite places to go in Beijing was the Grand Hotel near the Forbidden City. Part of the red brick building dated back to 1915. Although worn, I loved its old world feel and décor. I chose this location for meetings. I liked to eat lunch and dinner in the cavernous restaurant. I liked the Chinese food there as well as the bar. The service was good, unlike other places where people could care less how long you waited for anything.

Although I didn't see much of it, I knew that as a journalist I was being monitored in some ways by Chinese authorities. Envelopes I received in the mail had two stroke marks across the front: one in red and blue next to it. I was told these marks indicated mail had been read.

My uncle decided it would be nice to send me a box of chocolate truffles in Beijing for Valentine's Day. When I went to the Post Office to get them, I found the package had been opened. Someone had stuck their fingers into the bottom of each chocolate. It was very disgusting. Goo from the inside oozed in the package, which was beautifully wrapped just like my uncle would have done. The ribbon was perfectly in place, as was the wrapping paper. I opened the package at the Post Office, saw the ruined candy and became very angry. I walked over to the counter, showed what happened and yelled a tirade at the staff behind the counter. Shrugging their shoulders at me, they didn't care. I left, since I could do nothing. I let my uncle know. We both shared in the disappointment.

A market in Dalian (both pages). Photos by Noël-Marie Fletcher.

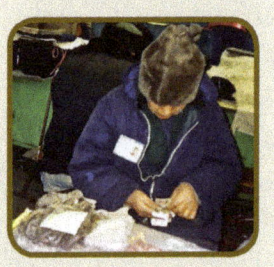

My phone was monitored. During a call to the States one afternoon, the person I was talking to set the phone down to answer the door. I sat there fuming in silence. The call was expensive. I thought she could attend to her business after I finished talking, but she stepped away. Within a few minutes, a Chinese woman's voice spoke on the line. She asked in Mandarin if I was finished talking on the phone. I couldn't believe it. I yelled at her to get off the phone because I was still using it. Eventually the person I was talking to picked up the phone on the other end. I finished my conversation shortly thereafter.

Before I moved to Beijing, I had acquired a great deal of

knowledge about the Boxer Rebellion. In 1900, many foreigners, especially Christian missionaries and their Chinese converts, were murdered by a group of Chinese called Boxers and the Qing Dynasty army. These killings to rid China of foreign occupants and influences happened throughout the country. An incident called the Siege of Peking occurred at the Beijing Legation Quarter, which underwent a 55-day attack until being rescued by a coalition of international military forces. I periodically drove to the Legation area in Beijing to shop and dine in restaurants. A huge store there sold temple stone rubbings. I bought many of these one afternoon while talking to staff about costumes worn by the ancients, Buddhist symbols and classic scenery that came to life through black ink on white rice paper.

A typical old Chinese neighborhood. In Beijing during the winter, people placed fresh cabbage atop the roofs of their low-level homes at the onset of the cold season. The cabbages remained chilled for months due to the cold weather outdoors. People took the cabbage off their roofs to cook when they wanted to eat it. Outdoor pollution and coal dust accumulated on the cabbages. Photo by Noël-Marie Fletcher.

Another historic site from the Boxer Rebellion was Beitang or the Church of the Savior. There Catholic missionaries and Chinese orphans sought shelter during the Siege of Peking. I attended Midnight Mass there one Christmas Eve. As a Catholic, I wanted to do something familiar to commemorate this important day. So I braved the cold and drove to the church, built in gothic style as a cathedral in the late 1880s. I was surprised to see crowds of Chinese people inside and outside. It felt like I was attending a sold-out concert. As I looked around, I noticed that few people seemed to be participating in the Mass. They looked more like gawking tourists taking in the sights. During the time I experienced strange nightmares in my apartment, I went to the church to get holy water to use in case my apartment was haunted. I have a photo of myself holding a jar of holy water outside this church.

My maternal grandparents Desolina Perea Candelaria and Carlos Candelaria on their wedding day. I was very close to my grandparents, who helped raise me. I learned to speak Spanish, their mother language, as my first language in their household where they cared for me from my infancy until my first school years. My grandparents remained a constant source of love in my life until their deaths. I exchanged many cards and letters with them during my years in Asia.

My grandfather Carlos before his death, which occurred during my time in Beijing. I spoke to him on the phone, even though he could no longer talk, to give him my love a few days before he died. Photo by Noël-Marie Fletcher.

My grandfather, whom I loved and admired, died during my time in Beijing. This was very tragic for me since he helped raise me after I was born. I felt helpless not being able to do anything during his final days. I went to the church to see if I could pay for a Mass to be offered for him. The Chinese priest didn't seem to know what to do. He wrote in Chinese characters on pieces of paper to pray for my grandfather and handed them out to people seated on the pews inside the church. I watched as the people took the slips of paper. I don't know whether anyone except me prayed for my dying grandfather but it made me feel better that I at least tried.

My encounters with ordinary Chinese people were limited when I lived in Beijing because I knew they could get in trouble for associating with a foreign journalist. I had a couple of Chinese friends who worked with me and other journalists as interpreters. I was always cautious when I went to their homes, which were very small, cramped and located in dilapidated *hutong* neighborhoods.

Train workers rest in China. Photo by Noël-Marie Fletcher.

One guy (I'll call Lyle) was a daring, handsome rascal. He lived with his family in a choice area due to its close proximity to the Forbidden City. His parents, who were much older than himself, spoiled him. He had been what was known as a change-of-life baby. He took many risks and loved it. His parents had joined the Communist Party before 1949, which he said made them viewed as more loyal and provided him with greater autonomy. His aged grandmother had bound feet. I never saw her. He was ashamed to discuss her at first. Having bound feet made her a victim of the previous cruel regime, and her plight underscored the need for a Communist revolution. This also resulted in generous treatment for Lyle.

Lyle told me a sad story about a mentally handicapped boy he went to elementary school with. One day the boy, whose mind was not all there, scribbled on the wall near the bathroom where he wrote Chairman Mao's name. Because the leader's name had been placed in such an undesirable location, school authorities punished the boy. He was taken from his family in Beijing and sent away, never to be seen again. When Lyle recalled witnessing this event, he became very emotional because he pitied the boy, who shouldn't have been held responsible since he didn't fully understand his action.

Bicycles outside a business in Beijing. Photo by Noël-Marie Fletcher.

Morning commute in Tianjin. Photo by Noël-Marie Fletcher.

I saw few Asian men with Caucasian girlfriends during my years in Hong Kong and China. Lyle, however, was an exception. He loved blondes and selected plenty of them from the pool of foreign exchange students. The affairs worked out for the college girls, who got to bed a handsome and charming Chinese guy, and it worked out for him since he liked their company and desired to leave the mainland for a bigger life elsewhere. Through his girlfriends, he made lots of future connections that he could tap into.

I invited friends over to my apartment frequently. I enjoyed listening to the latest music from America and the U.K., and always bought large batches of CDs and cassette tapes during my frequent flights to Hong Kong and annual trips to the States. I found ways to make food and share it with my friends. Liquor flowed under a haze of cigarette smoke. We cranked up the music, which my guests really enjoyed listening to since such music was unavailable in China.

The windy season in Beijing meant sand made its way into my apartment due to a lack of weather-stripping around the large glass windows. Sandstorms were so bad in Beijing that people draped thin scarves over their entire heads, which made them look like lollipop

Coal, a main energy source, outside a factory in northern China. Photo by Noël-Marie Fletcher.

people as they walked and rode bicycles around the city. During the horrendous sandstorms, the air was tinted a yellow shade like the color of curry.

A woman walks down a street during early winter in northern China. Photo by Noël-Marie Fletcher.

During winter, cold temperatures from outside crept right into my rooms. It was so cold I could hardly stand it. Someone told me to make a flour paste and stick thin sheets of packing paper on the windows as insulation. I did this. I also received advice to buy a humidifier to alleviate the dryness of the air in Beijing. I discovered this to be helpful also.

It was so dry during winter that it was easy to get static electricity shocks if you touched your fingertips to just about anything. Zap! The shocks were very sharp and painful. That happened all the time in the winter with everything you touched. I've never experienced this anywhere except during the dry winters in Beijing. After a few months with the humidifier on in my apartment, I noticed the flour paste I mixed became a haven for mold colonies. Off came the paper on the windows, in came more cold air.

I had no control over the heating in my apartment. The government turned on the heat at a designated date on the calendar (not changing even if cold temperatures had already arrived weeks before). There was nothing to be done but freeze until the heating date arrived. I couldn't turn the temperature up either. It was set to whatever the government thought it should be. I never knew what that mysterious number was, only that I froze in my apartment for several months, usually

Billboards in Beijing during the summer months. Photos (both pages) by Noël-Marie Fletcher.

from November until the spring came around April.

The same thing happened in the spring, when the government shut the heat off. The summer was awful for a few weeks when the government turned off the hot water. I was told this was to conserve energy. Cold showers aren't my thing. I had to boil water several times in a tea kettle to fill up my bathtub. Luckily, a swank gym at the Lido Hotel opened. It had a swimming pool and gym. I used to drive there for showers.

I looked forward to warm summer months. Most places had portable fans, few had central air conditioning unless you were in a large hotel. I carried a paper fan with me from the assortment that I had gotten as tourist souvenirs during my airplane travels. I also had a couple of sandalwood fans that exuded an aromatic scent when I used them.

Watermelons became a summer mainstay. I recall speaking with a Chinese girl in Beijing who was shocked that there were watermelons in America. She thought this fruit was a Chinese-only treat. Many Chinese viewed themselves as being special and China as the center of everything fine. I recall reading a newspaper article in Beijing that declared a Chinese person had actually discovered America, not Christopher Columbus.

I spoke to an older Chinese man once about overseas Chinese people, such as Americans of Chinese descent. He explained that a person is always considered Chinese no matter what land they are born on. "China is a tree. An overseas Chinese is a leaf. A leaf always falls to the ground where the tree is," he said.

Besides the non-exclusive-to-China origin of watermelons, the Chinese were puzzled by the meaning of my surname: Fletcher. I told them my surname had a meaning just like Chinese names. They found it very astounding. But the best part was when I told them what my surname meant—arrow maker. This really freaked them out. They looked at me strangely. Some were taken aback. Their expressions usually conveyed shock. They thought the meaning of my name was ominous and from a family with a lethal occupation. They didn't really like it at all. In Shanghai one businessman asked me about my name. When he heard its meaning, he became very apprehensive. "Don't shoot an arrow through me," he said with alarm.

Both myself and the people I interviewed turned over the business cards we'd exchanged after initial introductions. Many people couldn't read my English name. Instead they viewed my Chinese name Fang Ne and gave me compliments on what a great name it was. "This is good name for a Chinese person," I was told. Many foreigners had Chinese names that were nonsense and composed of characters that sounded like their English surnames. But I had a distinct Chinese name in addition to an interesting English name.

When the weather got warmer, I enjoyed looking out my apartment window onto an open park-like area. Sometimes I rose before sunrise. I'd make a cup of coffee, grab a cigarette, and stand in front of the window looking outside. Traffic was light. As the shadows of darkness lifted, I watched as blurry shapes became silhouettes of people. Outlines of forms gave way to scenes of people standing in the morning light. The limbs of dozens and dozens of men and women swayed and bent as they

The Great Wall of China. Photos by Noël-Marie Fletcher.

performed tai chi. It was the strangest thing to view. In the darkness, you couldn't see anyone there at all. Then as the daybreak sky turned from black to gray it looked like a crowd of zombies, who barely moved, stood in a throng. Only when light came could I see people exercising.

One of my favorite summer memories is of a night as darkness fell. I was walking to a restaurant to meet friends in one part of the city. I had parked my car and was going across the street. Then I heard an almost indescribable humming and buzzing sound that sounded like some strange sound effect from a cheesy 1950s monster movie. I turned toward this strange noise. In the darkness, I had trouble seeing anything on the street except a reed-thin man in light cotton clothes slowly pedaling a broken-down bicycle towards me. There was no other traffic on the road. I stood there, trying to figure out what the strange sound was that I could hear getting louder and louder. I had no idea what the noise could be. As the man on the bike approached me, I caught a glimpse of the load he struggled to convey. I saw he carried what appeared to be a thousand small bamboo cages, about the size of baseballs, with small hole openings. The cages were tied to each other to form a huge shape that rose above his head and hung over both sides of the back tire. Inside the cages were crickets. And these crickets were all making music together. The noise was incredible. I marveled at this.

I'm standing before an imperial throne.

I had heard that in ancient times the Chinese had house-pet and fighting varieties of crickets (like roosters) used for betting. I visited antique stores where they sold cricket cages, and I even bought one. Mine was like a drinking glass, only made of ceramic, that had a removable lid with holes in it. I also heard that people used to feed crickets lettuce and other green leafy things. I found this knowledge fascinating.

Warmer weather provided more enjoyable opportunities to view famous sights in Beijing. I visited the Great Wall of China—a real disappointment. It was such a tourist trap. People selling souvenirs everywhere. Camels were on hand to pose for souvenir photos. The worst part of it was climbing the steps of the wall as loudspeakers blared Michael Jackson songs. I had to turn my feet sideways while ascending and descending since my feet were too large to fit normally on the steps.

I visited the Forbidden City a few times. It was immense. If you think of it as a city, only then will you fully realize its immensity inside the walled enclosures. Lots of tourists from all over China visited the place. Most of the furnishings were gone when I saw it. Empty pavilions, halls, archways, and walkways looked like faded ghosts of a bygone time. It was like a city of outer shells with an emptiness inside. The buildings were cold. Before entering each one, you had to lift your feet to climb over an interior step. I was told these doorway barriers were to block evil from directly entering the rooms. It amazed me to see how far away (in what I viewed as a remote area) the concubines lived from the main areas. I was told there were secret walls and passages in some buildings. No doubt this was true. I loved looking at the magnificent architecture, especially the tiled roofs.

On the pavement were many squares containing images made of tiny pebbles. I found these little works of art to have an understated beauty. What could be a drab stone here and there was carefully arranged by color to form patterns and pictures. I found it very ingenious. Another thing that struck me was the different parallel walkways throughout the grounds. The center path with carved dragons was meant for the emperor. A path on each side of

Views of the Forbidden City. Photos by Noël-Marie Fletcher.

the imperial walkway could be used by various ministers and court officials. It was very exhilarating for me to be at such a beautiful historic place.

My two favorite places were the Temple of Heaven and the Summer Palace. The Temple of Heaven presented a spectacular sight. I found it a masterpiece of the beauty of Chinese art and culture. It has a circular wall built in tiers around the base. My Chinese friends told me that if you say something loud at the wall your sounds can be transmitted for a long distance because of the way the wall was built.

I also enjoyed my visit to the Summer Palace, which was just as crowded with Chinese tourists as the Forbidden City. The drive from Beijing to the Summer Palace was almost an hour. The place was a favorite spot for the last Empress Dowager. Because I had read a lot about its history and role in the Boxer Rebellion, I looked forward to viewing the

Chinese tourists at the Temple of Heaven in Beijing. Photo by Noël-Marie Fletcher.

The Summer Palace outside of Beijing. Leaves from lotus plants cover the waters (above). A young girl (below) at the Summer Palace. Photos by Noël-Marie Fletcher.

area. It was spectacular. It had a large white, two-story marble boat in a lake. There were many gardens, especially floating lotus gardens.

This was the first time I had seen lotus flowers, which I found exquisite. Near one area with lotus flowers, I paused to look around and saw a group of little old ladies with bound feet. They sat in the sun and seemed to be enjoying themselves. Their feet were as small in length as a deck of cards. A lot of walking was involved in visiting that site because it spanned a large area and buildings were located far apart. I could well imagine how these women were unable to walk around to see all the sights. It was probably best for them to remain in that central area among the crowds.

I enjoyed viewing the architecture and studying the symbols incorporated into the décor. However, I found that the place felt hollow, as if it were missing something, just as I felt at the Forbidden City.

Chapter 7: Paloma

After living in Beijing for nearly a year, I was lonely and wanted a dog. I researched it. However, I heard that Chinese people in Beijing and other large cities weren't allowed to have dogs due to fears of rabies. I never saw any dogs during my time in Beijing. In fact, only in rural areas in China and Hong Kong did I see ratty-looking chow dogs running around streets. Cats could be found in abundance, but I wanted a dog. I flew to Hong Kong to find out about a rescue dog. I knew a couple of journalists there who had adopted unwanted dogs. I discovered a rescue would not be an option. Dogs had to be sterilized prior to adoption and couldn't receive approval to fly until they had healed from surgery, which took several weeks.

I had always wanted a Dalmatian dog because I liked the way they looked. Another reason I liked them was due to a spotted dog being part of my father's Fletcher family crest. I decided to buy a Dalmatian puppy from a breeder in the San Francisco Bay area.

Prior to having the puppy flown out to me in Beijing, I went to the local government office and met with various officials to gain approval. They thought I was out of my mind. It was unconventional for a foreigner to do that, and the government officials acted like they thought it would be good fun to assist in such an acquisition.

Without much hassle, I had everything under control. The female puppy left San Francisco and traveled to Beijing via Tokyo. I drove to the airport and waited in an office with about three government officials. We all shared an eagerness to see the puppy. They didn't know what type of dog it was, only that it was an American puppy.

Baby Paloma and I pause outside an embassy while on a walk near my apartment in Beijing.

After a short wait, one worker brought my puppy in a container. The dog was so cute. She had lovely markings. At that age, she lacked all of her black spots, which appeared more as she grew up. Her coat was a soft white with small black flecks like beauty marks. Everyone gathered around her, petting the dog, making admiring remarks. I wanted a Spanish name. I mulled over several options before deciding on the name Paloma (meaning "dove"), which I thought was a good choice for a little girl dog.

My forms received official approval in red chop marks from a Chinese seal. I drove Paloma to her new home in my apartment. I hadn't realized until she was en route to me that no dogs in Beijing meant no dog food could be found in stores. Hmmmmm. I wondered what to do. I knew that Chinese people fed their cats steamed white rice with bits of meat in it. I thought this was too strange. I didn't want to raise my dog on a rice diet so I created a protein diet of eggs, meat and some vegetables.

My maid was excited to have a puppy. She got instant celebrity status among all the other maids in the building. Often she asked for permission to take the dog for a walk. I had no problem with that. People gathered around her when she took Paloma out. She became an expert on the dog, chatting to people in the building (residents, maids and the surly maintenance workers on the ground floor) to share lots of details about the creature.

Another fact that eluded me before Paloma's arrival was how her breed would surprise people. Dalmatians were unknown in Beijing. Crowds always gathered around me when I took her on walks as well as when I drove around with her

Paloma rests in my bedroom in Beijing. Photo by Noël-Marie Fletcher.

in the car. She attracted a lot of attention.

I soon found that strangers knew about me because of my dog. Chinese people didn't at first really realize she was a dog. Many people approached me to see the strange "cow." Children squealed with excitement when they saw Paloma. People cautiously approached me to get a closer look. They didn't want to get bitten. Once a unsavory-looking young man, who looked like he belonged in a triad criminal organization, ran across a park where Paloma and I were walking. He wore oddly shaped dark sunglasses with mirrored lenses. He pulled out his wallet, offering me $100 in U.S. dollars to buy Paloma. I knew it was an incredible amount of money for a local Beijing person to have. Also the fact that he had U.S. dollars was nearly as unheard of, making me fairly certain he was some kind of hoodlum. Also, I didn't know how he thought he was going to own a dog since it was illegal for Chinese to do so in Beijing. I refused his offer. I had no interest in selling my beloved dog. The guy left very disappointed and deflated.

Paloma was a sweetheart. She was the goofiest dog. She loved people, especially children. If she saw a baby, she pulled really hard on the leash for me to take her to visit children. Her biggest problem was bladder control. When people petted her, Paloma often became so excited that she urinated on the spot. Then her wagging tail sprayed it all over the place. This was extremely problematic in the elevator to my apartment. I hated for anyone to pet her in the elevator because a puddle would appear.

I lived on the 11th floor and started taking the stairs to avoid this problem. Going down was fine as she bounded down the stairs. The climb was a struggle for us both. She didn't want to go up. I had to make a few stops to catch my breath.

When the weather became warmer in the summer time, I had an unexpected surprise. Paloma was sniffing like a bloodhound through a patch of long grass near my apartment where foreign embassies were located. While looking down and watching her, I saw a black bug streak across her white fur only to disappear into one of her black spots. I crouched down to examine her fur. I'd never seen a flea in my life until then. It was shocking to realize that she had these and that I also had nowhere to buy flea powder. I dragged her home and threw her in the bathtub to drown whatever fleas I could locate. With water flung all over the floor and walls, we were both soaked. I could see that some fleas died.

In a panic, I talked to some of my journalist friends. We agreed something had to be done. Luckily my apartment only had one area carpet, and mostly tile floors. Someone told me garlic would do the trick until I could fly to Hong Kong to buy flea repellent. I bought lots and lots of garlic that I fed to the dog, who'd eat almost anything. I don't know if the garlic repelled fleas, but it sure worked on people. That dog smelled like a garlic bomb. She positively glowed. It was horrible. Every time I opened the door to enter my apartment, I was hit in the face by an overpowering smell of garlic and dog. I think it made her dog odor worse besides adding a stench of garlic. Combing the dog plus frequent bathing and the garlic seemed to work for a week until I could leave for Hong Kong.

When Paloma was about six months old, she developed allergies in her ears. The poor dog really suffered. She constantly shook her ears, which became red inside and very puffy. I didn't know what to do. I consulted anyone who would listen to me to try to find a solution.

Eventually, through word of mouth, I learned about a Chinese veterinarian who lived in Beijing. He spoke no English, which was a challenge since my vocabulary in Mandarin didn't include many words about dogs and allergies. The vet appeared to be in his 70s. His office was the front room of his tiny ground-floor apartment. His trade primarily consisted of treating pet cats, which kept him busy since he was the only vet in Beijing anyone knew about. Before World War II, he had been educated in Japan as a veterinarian. Somehow he survived the war and the Cultural Revolution. Despite being very thin and frail, he worked. No retirement for him.

He refused to touch Paloma without a muzzle. I told him how friendly she was, but he didn't care. I explained that I had no muzzle. Not a problem. He whipped out a long, dirty gray-colored soft cord that he tied around her mouth. He did this every time he saw her thereafter. I learned how to tie it myself. You place the cord over the top of the dog's nose with the strings hanging down on each side of the jaw. Then you cross the cord under the jaw, bringing each string to one side of the neck. At the base of the neck, the strings tie together in a bow. It worked fine. From then on, I always knew how to fashion a muzzle for a dog from a piece of cord or rope.

Paloma grows up in Beijing. Photo by Noël-Marie Fletcher.

The vet mixed his own prescriptions. He had a section of the room with medicinal powders and small squares of white paper. After examining Paloma's ears, he retreated across the room, busying himself with measuring teaspoonfuls of beige powder. The medicine was placed in the center of a piece of paper, which was then folded carefully around all sides to keep the contents in place. It almost looked like he was folding origami paper triangles. He explained to me how much powder to give her each day. The medicine helped keep her allergies under control, but she suffered from them throughout her life and often saw the vet.

I almost got shot by an embassy military guard one day while walking Paloma outside for a walk. I used to take the dog along the same streets around my apartment compound for long walks to give her exercise and allow her to do her business. We often passed the same embassies day after day. Each embassy had a Chinese armed soldier standing guard in front. Most of the time, the soldiers were young reed-thin men who looked bored out of their minds. They never spoke. They just stood there with their guns. I always ignored them.

One afternoon, one of these soldiers began to harass Paloma as we walked by. He kept shouting at her, making noises, trying to scare her with threatening gestures. I tried to ignore him but he was being a jerk. He didn't act like anyone surprised to see a Dalmatian. His attitude was belligerent and his behavior threatening.

I lost my temper. I had been taught a curse word in Mandarin that meant "turtle egg." I was warned not to use it carelessly because it was so offensive. I decided to hurl that word at the soldier. He leapt from his post and came running straight at me with his gun aimed. He was so enraged I could see him trembling. His face flushed red. Still angry, I turned my back to him, sauntering sassily away with my dog. I thought if I said anything else to him I would've been shot on the spot. It was best to act like I didn't have a care in the world as I sashayed away while he yelled at me. I knew I had a close call that day. I also knew it really was a bad word—just as I'd been told. I never used that curse word again.

Easily one of the prettiest pets I've ever had, Paloma lacked in the brains department. She had a great personality, but did a lot of dumb things. For instance, she loved to bite the blossoms of flowers off while walking past them. She'd act like she didn't see a lovely flower in bloom. Then suddenly as we approached, she dive bombed it like a hawk, grabbing the petals between her teeth, tossing her head to the side and letting it fall to the ground. I didn't like this, and neither did the owners of those garden flowers. Sometimes this nasty business had consequences for her. Bees. Yep, they'd be happily frolicking among the petals only to find themselves inside her pink mouth with black

Paloma rolls in the grass in Beijing during her walk. Photo by Noël-Marie Fletcher.

spots. Of course, they stung her all over her tongue and other areas in her mouth.

My apartment in Beijing had some inferior type of white coating like interior wall paint. Paloma found it very tasty. If I didn't keep a close eye on her or shut certain doors, I'd find her contentedly licking the white stuff off the wall.

She also liked to gallop around without heeding any commands. A few times, she broke away from my grasp on her leash while we were outdoors. The compound was inside a brick wall enclosure and had armed guards in booths at the entrances. I don't know if she realized she was free or if she decided, "Hey, this is fun." She bounced and flounced going this way and that as I screamed out her name, running after her. When she stopped to sniff something, which she often did, I'd grab her.

The only other foreigners I knew in Beijing who had dogs were the U.S. Ambassador's wife (hers was a small handbag-type of dog) and the wife of another foreign journalist (she had a clumsy golden retriever). After the Tiananmen massacre and crackdown, I took Paloma on the last U.S. flight evacuated from Beijing. I left her with my relatives in New Mexico and returned to Beijing. When I left China for good in October 1989, I was reunited with Paloma in the United States and took her to live with me in Los Angeles.

Paloma sleeps in Beijing. Photo by Noël-Marie Fletcher.

Chapter 8: Journalist Community

The community of journalists in Beijing was varied, representing the world's leading countries. The group I associated with were the English-speaking ones—Canadians, Australians, British, and Americans. Because the press corps in Beijing was relatively small, people tended to see one another and know other reporters even if they didn't run in the same crowd. For example, Agence France-Presse had its office in one of the diplomatic compounds. So if you went into that building sooner or later you'd run into one of the French news agency's reporters. I filed my stories to Phil in Hong Kong from a wire service office on the ground floor of another diplomatic compound down the street from mine. Phil then sent my stories to the foreign desk in New York City.

While living in Beijing, I only hung around with journalists. Although reporters often have sources who provide them information on a regular basis, many journalists really feel comfortable and let their hair down when being among others in the news business. You don't have sources trying to use you or manipulate coverage, or act like they have a reporter in their hip pocket. You can relax with other journalists, who tend to be interested in the same sorts of things—adventure, writing, telling interesting stories, traveling, etc. Journalists also can be gossipy, nosy people. Since we all lived and worked in the same general areas, we often ran into each other. There were less than a dozen restaurants in Beijing that everyone frequented. Similarly, there were only a couple of places where foreigners shopped for groceries and consumer goods.

The U.S. Embassy had its own grocery store in Beijing, but Americans couldn't shop there unless they were diplomats or invited by a diplomat. I never set foot in there.

I decided it would be fun to pose for a Christmas card photo I would create. I found a great spot next to an imperial stone lion guardian in front of the Forbidden City, facing Tiananmen Square. I had two floral hair ornaments (one red, one white) that looked like pom-poms. I fastened these to white and red T-shirts, which I wrapped around my head to look like elf hats. Then I posed for a series of photos in front of a tripod. I'm also wearing the warm, heavy fur coat I bought in Shanghai.

I bought most of my food at the Friendship Store down the street where most other foreigners and some Chinese shopped. It had a small grocery section about the size of those inside gas stations. The brands were all Chinese. There were canned fruit, some frozen items (fish or whole chickens with the legs and heads sticking out of the plastic), condiments (like soy sauce), eggs with bird excrement and feathers on them, and fresh vegetables. Finding things to cook could be a challenge.

A European joint-venture bakery and butcher store opened up across town. That was another place foreigners went to shop. I usually encountered a journalist when I visited there. Eventually another foreign-joint venture opened that provided meat. I'd phone in an order, which was delivered to my apartment. The only requirement was that you had to order a large quantity of meat. That wasn't a problem since I could freeze it.

If I went to a store to buy groceries, I could meet up with someone walking in my compound later in the day. During the conversation, I'd mention that I had gotten groceries and the other person would reply that they'd heard so already from someone else. The journalist community was that small.

Sometimes journalists slept around with each other's

partners—giving rise to scandal and bad blood. One night I was with a group of journalists chatting. Among the group was a woman reporter. She had been lonely and in need of male companionship. So she began a relationship with a male reporter she didn't really like. She was in it for the fun. She giddily told everyone that she'd come home unexpectedly to her apartment only to find this "boyfriend" wearing her clothes, including her bra. She shrieked with laughter. She described all the little details about this occurrence. None of us could believe it. We were completely scandalized. We didn't really know the person that well and didn't generally like him either. She told us with great excitement about how she dumped him. He became a laughingstock.

The Friendship Store (above) was one of the main places I bought consumer items and groceries in Beijing. I discovered a lifelong love of jasmine body soap during my time in China because it was plentiful there. Photo by Noël-Marie Fletcher.

We journalists in Beijing were wards of the Foreign Ministry. They had minders assigned to each nationality. The ones for Americans spoke English with an American accent. Those in charge of the British had upper-class English accents. At that time, there were two American journalists who had dark hair and beards, and wore eyeglasses. These two guys looked dissimilar to Western eyes. However their Chinese Foreign Ministry minders could never figure out which one was which. They would intend to yell at one of them, call the wrong guy in, and start yelling at him. They couldn't tell the difference between the two. They thought both men looked identical. It got to be a standing joke.

Clothing available at high-end local stores for foreigners in China. Photo by Noël-Marie Fletcher.

I was among the founding members of the Foreign Correspondents Club of Beijing that set itself up informally in part of an American hotel there. Arrangements were made to have one part of the hotel serve food for us in front of large TVs where we could watch the news. It wasn't live but had been taped a few hours earlier. That's how we got to watch U.S. TV news. We all had an FCC party one night. Part of the entertainment consisted of a skit called, "Two Men in Beards." Both the American guys with glasses and beards danced around stage together laughing and joking about being mistaken for twins. We all found it very amusing.

There were unspoken distinctions among the foreign journalists about who the "real" journalists were. Some people became foreign correspondents because they went to a fancy school and learned to speak Mandarin. Others came up through the news ranks, didn't speak much Mandarin, and had been promoted through their hard work to the coveted spot as China correspondent. The "China expert" academic-type "journalists," whose qualifications were language skills rather than news, were often looked down on by those who really had the education, training and experience of being professional journalists with track records of working in the news business.

Most people presume that all journalists see the news business in the same way and behave similarly. That's not true—particularly in view of jobs at big news outfits and cushy overseas correspondent gigs. People from fancy schools don't really get jobs working in the trenches of news—those small-town newspapers or TV stations with vicious politicians, corrupt public officials, indifferent regulators, celebrity nobodies and business leaders who think they own the town.

Journalists who start in those less prestigious (sometimes undesirable) places, while working up the food chain of news, get to know all the dirty tricks (and job challenges) that surface later in big-time, high-profile news environments. You've seen it happen before but with less sophisticated (and sometimes less intelligent) players, who all behave in similar ways (lusting for power, wealth, or sex) and who try to use the news to suit their own agendas.

If you are a journalist experienced in dealing with these dark players, you are better able to sift through manipulation, lies, bribes, and "off-the-record" knife-in-someone-else's-back tactics. You've already been burned by some people. You've had good editors save you from mistakes, and warn you about people and situations. You've used journalism tools to force officials to give you the information you are entitled to have in our free American society. Many newsrooms I worked in early in my career had stickers on all telephones to call for free legal advice if people were withholding records and other public documents. I phoned these lawyers often to get advice, particularly when I was a court reporter, covering police beats and negotiating with authorities who wanted to withhold public information. That's one way I learned what documents I had a right to demand, how police try to hide their reports, and how officials can twist information into being reported as credible news by uninformed or lazy journalists, who let others interpret or spoon-feed them information.

Public transportation. Photo by Noël-Marie Fletcher.

If you are freshly minted from an expensive fancy school on a fast-track conveyor belt to a big job in a big town, you probably haven't been bruised from the trench warfare of small-town news or battle tested for high-stakes fights. This inexperienced, over-indulged type of reporter is likely to become a pawn in a chess game or want to become a player in the game—

rather than an objective observer telling people what is really going on.

There is already a danger in the news business of reporters believing they are special because they're treated differently when their name is in the newspaper or their face is on a TV screen or they have a zillion social media followers. It can be a big ego boost. A news platform provides journalists with public visibility that can be used for the good of society or as a mechanism to puff oneself up into an elite guru, who plys personal wisdom, political rants, humor, and insights—book deals come their way, interviews for their expert opinions, public-speaking engagements. Followers encircle them as a cult of personality forms. The standard news format used to be an inverted pyramid (the most important information on the top, the least at the bottom) instead of today's narcissistic "look at me, this is what I think" musings that are passed off as news.

Today's forms of "journalism" result from reporters who are really diarists writing about nothing newsworthy and lifestyle-political pundits who advocate the proper us-versus-them way to think about people and events. Gone in many places is the journalism that gives witness to history.

I recently attended a press conference in Washington, D.C. at the National Press Club. A public political figure was speaking. I was shocked by the "questions" posed by the throng of journalists. There were long-winded preambles by reporters…I kept waiting to hear an actual question that

My T-shirt from the Foreign Correspondents Club of Beijing, China. I was a founding member of the FCC of China—the first professional association of foreign journalists working in the People's Republic of China. I was honored to be part of this. Photo by Noël-Marie Fletcher.

came several minutes after pontificating, posturing, and grandstanding. This took time away from other reporters, who could have asked legitimate news questions during the allotted period. Instead, only a few windbags had a chance to announce their self-aggrandized musings to the public figure. One reporter tried to speak as some kind of insider, in what didn't sound like a question but a shared memory or story that let everyone in the room know how the two were buddies. Another reporter announced himself using three types of titles; normally, reporters merely state their name and news affiliation prior to asking a question. However, this person rattled off something like a job description to imply his personal importance. Unbelievable. This also took time away from other potential questions. Another reporter asked a question in a snarky way that reeked of personal political bias. In no way did this resemble my training about how true journalists (representing the public rather than personal interest) should conduct themselves.

Some foreign journalists came to China to make a name for themselves—gain a career-changing notch on their belt. I saw plenty of that type—those who care nothing about people, but only collect persons they find useful. They move from person to person at events, sniffing around to catch a parasitic scent of potential hosts to feed upon. Some of these ambitious journalists appeared to lack a conscience—caring nothing for other journalists, press freedom issues, nor the Chinese people they reported about. Instead they sought news platforms to stand upon to be worshiped as sages.

The career path for China correspondents could involve future prestigious postings in Tokyo, at the White House, or in New York City. Some could refine the exotic expertise of being in Asia and become a "China Hand" journalist. I saw many China correspondents rarely set foot outside their posts in Beijing. They got their news from rewriting stories published by Chinese reporters in Chinese newspapers or those that aired on Chinese TV. While that is a legitimate way to get news, it also is a lazy way to skew "news" by only rehashing the party line from government-sanctioned news organizations. Local cultures and people are viewed with smug disdain by this type of lazy, out-of-touch foreign correspondent, which is still very prevalent today. Sadly, I witnessed it recently while covering news in Berlin.

Other types of upwardly mobile "journalists" I encountered in Hong Kong and Beijing were foreign journalism interns—rich kids from swank schools who swanned into town, eagerly hung around newsrooms, sometimes with a parent paving their way. One journalism student intern I knew in Beijing liked to sleep around finding news to share with her editor. I'll call her Roberta. She passed along the info gained from pillow talk while the news appeared under her editor's name. He laughed once as he told everyone about how mad an ambassador became at him for breaking a story. The ambassador demanded to know the source. "If he only knew it was one of his military guards talking while in bed with Roberta," the editor declared. I can't recall Roberta ever working on a news story or having one appear under her own name. But she did continue her "career" in journalism after she left China with a good recommendation from her editor, who broke news derived from her bedroom activities with potential sources.

There wasn't much to do for fun in Beijing after you saw the tourist sights. Our social life centered on drinking parties in each other's apartments, going out for meals at local hotels and neighborhood restaurants, maybe watching a Chinese movie with English subtitles held infrequently at one hotel, and going to a foreign-joint venture gym for exercise (swimming, racquet ball, bowling, tennis).

A group of Argentinian diplomat wives became entrepreneurs by running a video rental business in their living room within my diplomatic compound. People had nothing to do so they rented movies that could be viewed alone or in groups. One American journalist had elderly parents in New York. They lovingly recorded his favorite TV shows on VHS tapes that they mailed to him. He'd phone me when the tapes arrived. A group of us got together to watch the shows. It was a real treat.

Another pastime we enjoyed was driving out to a shooting range in Beijing. A group of us journalists would assemble in cars and drive for about half an hour to the shooting range. We had a blast—literally. The Chinese would let you shoot off anything from their arsenal for a price. One journalist came back to where we were firing our weapons. He was laughing hysterically. He had just been informed that for an extra price he could shoot live chickens. Instead he opted to shoot off mortars. I liked to fire from pistols and the Chinese equivalents of AK-47s and M16s.

Once a French restaurant opened in Beijing where the food was fancy and expensive. I liked to go there to party with some of my American journalist friends. Often we saw French journalists there. My favorite drink at that time was a Brandy Alexander with extra nutmeg. It was not unusual for me to drink several, one after another, during an evening. I had

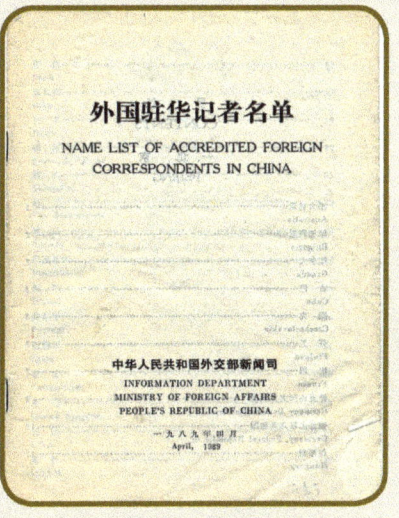

Listed within this booklet were journalists from only 27 countries that were officially accredited foreign correspondents authorized to work in China. I was among only 7 women reporters and 29 male journalists in the press corps who worked for American news organizations. Not every reporter in the U.S. press corps was American; some were British. The Foreign Affairs Ministry misspelled my first name. Photos by Noël-Marie Fletcher.

developed a high tolerance to alcohol from my nights at the Foreign Correspondents' Club in Hong Kong. The custom was to walk in and order a drink for your friends as you passed them by as a greeting. Some Friday nights I'd find myself with up to seven gin and tonics lined up for me. Most of the men drank beer, which I can't stand. Thankfully the FCC had food that could be ordered to mitigate the flowing liquor.

After dinner one night at the French restaurant, my group (which included a few American journalist men) decided to continue the fun with cocktails. The men were offered cigars. I ordered another Brandy Alexander and lit up my cigarette. Two Chinese girls came over with cigars and brandy, which the men indicated they wanted. In an elaborate ritual to prepare cigars for the men in my group, the girls acted as though they were having oral sex with the cigars. They were rolling them around putting the tips near their lips, etc. I became outraged. I thought it was disgusting, and I was insulted by this lewd behavior going on in front of me. I thought the girls were putting on this show for the men. I wondered if they'd do the same for me if I ordered a cigar. So I did just that. I demanded a cigar right then and there.

"Where's mine?" I asked. "You think men are the only ones who smoke cigars? Are you going to do that to my cigar?" I demanded.

The Chinese girls looked dumbfounded, exchanging confused looks at each other. They prepared my cigar—without the show. As I grabbed my cigar, everyone in my group was silent. The women said nothing and neither did the men. I stabbed my cigarette out and put the cigar in my mouth as if I'd smoked cigars a million times before. In reality, it was my first time, although I loved the smell of cigars and still do.

My companions stared as I took my first puff. The guys had theirs held between their teeth. I just about died since I deeply inhaled it like a cigarette—rather then exhaling swirling smoke puffs. I thought I'd turn green. But I held my own. I was

Since Beijing was a national capital city, many important events with dignitaries took place there, which provided ample  determined not to choke or show any discomfort. I learned to smoke it from watching the guys. To make my point, I smoked about half of it before I gave it up. Then I downed more liquor to get the taste out of my mouth and returned to smoking my cigarettes. None of my group reacted to my cigar-smoking stint. Maybe I pulled it off well.

material for news coverage. These photos of are of a Chinese trade fair at a Beijing hotel that I covered for my newspaper. Photos by Noël-Marie Fletcher.

The types of news as covered in a nation's capital city is pretty similar from one country to another. The focus is mostly on the central government—national politics, regulation, the economy, elections, industry, and the interactions of foreign countries. My news coverage once I moved to Beijing had the same macro focus, except my beat also had business, finance, trade, joint ventures, plus interactions with the American companies and officials since my newspaper was in New York City.

I did travel outside Beijing for news coverage, but not very often since my responsibility was to provide news coverage of an entire country rather than local sites. I liked to go to Shanghai and went there a few times for fun rather then work.

One day I got tremendous "face" in front of my male news competitors who sometimes looked down on me or acted as if I didn't exist. The World Bank president was holding a press conference. When I introduced

My desk in my Beijing apartment. I had airline tickets, books, files, an early computer, and kitchen bowls that I used as ashtrays and paper weights. Photo by Noël-Marie Fletcher.

myself to ask a question, the president greeted me very warmly. "This is great! I just had lunch with your publisher the other day." I could tell by the looks on their faces that they didn't like this public acknowledgement of me or my newspaper.

One challenge of being a foreign correspondent in a capital city comes from press conferences. It's hard to get an exclusive story when 50 other people are in the same room, hearing the same presentation of information, getting the same press packets, meeting the same source. If you are selected to ask a question during a press conference, all the other reporters can hear both what you want to know (giving them an idea of your interests) and the answer to your question. Often the best ways is to keep your question to yourself and pull the presenter aside at the end to try to ask questions privately.

Many times at press conferences, I also took photos to accompany my articles. This was unusual since there is normally no crossover between photojournalists and reporters. Not many reporters can also take photos professionally. This is still true even today.

Taking photos at press conferences (pressers) can present a monkey-see, monkey-do response from other photographers. They don't want you to get a better shot. So they cram right next to you, or take the place you were just standing in, to try to replicate your photo. I find it very silly, but many photojournalists do it.

Most news organizations monitor how your coverage stacks up against your competitors. It's great to break news and do a better job than your peers when you're going toe-to-toe. However, there are times when you will get beaten, too.

In China, some foreign correspondents (Americans included) coveted their relationships with diplomats at their embassies. Not me. I didn't like what I found. I had believed that the U.S. embassy had a primary responsibility to assist Americans with basic needs. Yet, my only basic need ever met by the U.S. embassy was to have pages added to my passport. My frequent travels resulted in all my pages being stamped by different countries before the expiration date of my passport. So I had to have pages added.

After I first moved to Beijing, I went to the commercial section of the U.S. Embassy to introduce myself to the staff there. All they wanted to do was play games with me to find out information. They didn't assist much at all in providing any useful information to me (in a public affairs capacity) that I could use. If I wanted to interview an American company or find out what type of joint ventures were going on with U.S. companies, I'd have more luck finding out for myself. The second time I went into the commercial section, one of the embassy workers there started asking me questions about where I'd gone, who I'd met, what I'd seen.

"Why are you asking me this?" I replied. "If you want to know something, can't you go drive around and figure it out for yourself?"

Taken aback, he retorted that it wasn't as easy as that. He said the Chinese tended to follow the U.S. diplomats around more than journalists. So that's why he appreciated information from journalists. We had more freedom of movement. I told him I was a journalist and not in the business of providing him with information. If he wanted to know something, he could find out on his own. After that I stayed as far away from U.S. Embassy personnel as possible.

One 4th of July, I responded to a flyer seeking American volunteers for an Independence Day celebration. I often I enjoy volunteering for events. I decided to lend a hand. The U.S. Embassy was flying in fast-food chain hamburgers into Beijing for a parade. I volunteered to hand out burgers. I had a grand time. These burgers had come from Hong Kong because they weren't available in China. I remember giving one to an American college student who had flown in from the hinterland. He was overjoyed to eat the hamburger. He hadn't had one in a couple of years. He said it was like having a little bit of home again. Although it was a hot, sunny day, the American community put on a parade that went past the burger stand. People dressed up in costumes, laughing, enjoying patriotic spirit, and being American together. I'm glad I volunteered. Otherwise I probably would've avoided the Embassy event and missed the fun.

Movie posters outside a theater in China. I used to attend Chinese movies with English subtitles in Beijing. Photos by Noël-Marie Fletcher.

The only other celebration I attended at the U.S. Embassy was a Halloween party a couple of weeks after I moved to Beijing. I knew no one. It didn't help that people were dressed in costumes, so I really couldn't tell who people really were. After the

Tiananmen massacre, the Chinese military shot into an apartment where the head of U.S. Embassy security lived with his family. I didn't know who he was. I was told that I met him—he was Dracula at the Halloween party.

Small children and their teachers walk along a busy street in Guangzhou. Photo by Noël-Marie Fletcher.

Some male foreign correspondents dated and married Chinese women. I'm sure not all alliances were to gain a foreign passport, but some cases sure seemed this way. I heard a story about one Chinese woman who married a foreign reporter. She had described how her family elders decided to take strategic measures to ensure their family survived the political turmoil after the fall of the last dynasty in the early 1900s. It was decided that one son would enter the military, another would become an academic, and the third would join the government. That way the family would have someone on an inside track no matter what happened within the country. The plan worked.

When it came to her generation of grandchildren, she was told she must marry an American to give the family a foothold in the United States, which she did. I saw many young giggling Chinese girls congregate in groups in places that foreigners frequented, such as cafes, rather than bars. I wondered if any of them had any similar instructions about what type of background to find in a spouse.

Chapter 9:
Tiananmen Square

I witnessed the expansion of foreign influences within China as the central government encouraged economic development and openness to overseas trade. Within the span of a few years, I saw the Chinese people gravitate toward the wonders of modernization and commercialism. For the most part, these things came from the West—America, in particular. The Chinese didn't just want any old thing. They wanted the best. I spoke to some young people about tennis shoes. They didn't want inexpensive brands, which would be more within their reach due to pricing. No, they wanted the top brands that cost the equivalent of several months' earnings for a single pair.

In Beijing, I saw the Chinese being introduced to American fast-food chicken, cola, TV shows, pop music, cartoon characters, and clothing. The younger people—particularly college students who started the Tiananmen Square movement—wanted it all and more. It was only natural that they also would seek Western democratic ideals.

I was in Hong Kong when Hu Yaobang died April 15, 1989. An off-and-on-again political leader, he had been a key player in China's early Communist history. His career as a high-ranking political official was notable. He had been a comrade of Chairman Mao, one of the youngest of the Long March veterans. At the time of his death, he had fallen from favor due to infighting over his economic reforms. I had been acting as a tour guide for my uncle and cousin in Southeast Asia. Our stop in Hong Kong was a short one before I brought them with me to Beijing to show them some sights in China.

When I returned to Beijing a few days after Hu's death, I heard about students protesting. I didn't think much of it. I didn't think it would go anywhere. I didn't think the government would put up with that kind of thing. But nothing happened to the students. With each passing day, they grew in number.

I went to Tiananmen Square several times to witness the movement. It was difficult to find parking nearby. People, mostly young students, were encamped all over, some in tents. The open public area acquired a lived-in atmosphere—the way a fairground looks during a week-long event when throngs of people have left their mark with discarded trash and other assorted debris.

Students form a line outdoors in Shanghai. Photo by Noël-Marie Fletcher.

All the foreign correspondents in Beijing were closely monitoring and reporting on this unfolding event. In normal circumstances, I'd see my journalist friends informally while out shopping, during dinners, or in casual encounters in a hotel lobby. Much of our lives involved coming and going from hotels to meet people, eat, buy newspapers or other imported small items from a gift shop, etc. There weren't many other places to congregate. If you were grabbing a tuna sandwich and fries at a hotel restaurant for a quick lunch, chances were high you'd see at least one other journalist you knew at the hotel or in the parking lot.

However, things changed once the protests started. Everyone was on 24-hour notice every day—day after day—without any conceivable end in sight. Interest was intense from my newspaper editors. Instead of being on the phone every week or so and relying on electronic messaging between us, I reported at least once a day and then more often as the situation unfolded. I'm sure this was the same case with every other journalist in Beijing as the Tiananmen Square movement took on a life of its own.

I still saw some of my friends here and there. We discussed our thoughts and shared information about what we had seen. It was harder for single reporters representing a news organization

Chinese youths in Beijing. Photo by Noël-Marie Fletcher.

to cover this. The wire services had teams of reporters so they could, and did, rotate people in and out of the square, while also sending reporters to talk to others outside the square.

The way it works in big news operations is that the foreign bureaus in closest proximity to where the action is provide backup support in a breaking news event. I remember there was a breaking news event in Pakistan that required backup reporters from Beijing to be flown in as reinforcements. In the case of the events at Tiananmen Square, the first place of backup for many news organizations was Hong Kong, followed by Tokyo. There were fears that the Chinese government would not recognize Hong Kong Chinese journalists as British subjects in case of an emergency at the square, and Hong Kong Chinese journalists could be arrested or harmed. One news organization drew its backup reinforcements from Japan to protect its Hong Kong Chinese journalists.

After a couple of weeks came the arrival of a class of journalists I call "news raptors"—foreign reporters, photographers, and TV anchors who suddenly fly into places where significant breaking news is occurring to deliver reportage from that area as if they're "the experts". This type of grandstanding journalist swaggers into a town, gets spoon-fed information about what is going on, and then tries to push away the boots-on-the-ground journalists, who have a deeper understanding about the reality of an event due to being based there or prior experience.

I've seen it happen at different big news events. These limelight seekers may represent a more prominent news outlet so their (often superficial) reporting of events captures a greater spotlight than that of a journalist who knows more. As soon as the spotlight moves to a different place, these news raptors are the first ones to leave town. Then months later, they are nominated for journalism awards.

Another type of "journalist" also arrived in Beijing that I'll refer to as wannabes. These reporters and photographers want to be in the business. They will freelance to whoever will pay. They take stupid risks. Some aren't even journalists at all. They pick up a notebook or camera and charge ahead seeking fame and fortune in danger zones. Smart journalists with experience know that they can report on events without being where bullets are flying. Usually they get up high over an event—like a window seat from a hotel—or become embedded with different parties at an event (like accompanying the military). As the number of protestors swelled at Tiananmen there was one foreign TV news outfit that took up a few hotel rooms with the best views. Then other news outlets likewise rented hotel rooms.

Part of Tiananmen Square facing the Great Hall of the People. Photo by Noël-Marie Fletcher.

Within a couple of weeks, tons of journalists from all over the world were running back and forth to report on the student protests at Tiananmen. People were flying in and out. Hotel rooms were being taken. The worldwide demand for reporting increased.

It was difficult for me to see some of my journalist friends who lived in Beijing. Everyone

Inside the Great Hall of the People. Many events I attended as a foreign correspondent in Beijing were held there. Photo by Noël-Marie Fletcher.

Chinese tourists pose for a funny photo at a display. Photo by Noël-Marie Fletcher.

was under pressure to stay on top of the evolving situation. The ones who were one-man news shops shared information with their friends to try to extend their reach to better assess the situation. Lots of us journalists who lived in Beijing were sharing information, such as:

- What was happening at the square.
- Where we saw military troops in the city.
- Which journalists were still at the square.
- Who had gone back to their home or office to report on the event or rest.

It was a very demanding time. My relatives in the States were alarmed by what they saw in the news. I had to field phone calls to let people know I was okay. My hometown TV news station somehow found out I was in Beijing. I did a phone interview with them late one night from my apartment, which was located very near Tiananmen Square. Pressure was building on professional and personal levels for most every journalist I knew in Beijing.

During this turmoil, I recall having dinner with an Australian journalist and his pregnant wife. They both had been threatened at gunpoint by the Chinese military.

I wasn't much of a tour guide for my relatives, who were still visiting me during the expansion of the protest movement (including a hunger strike by some students). My uncle and cousin found themselves in the midst of a city focused on activities on the square.

My Time in Another World

It was very difficult to drive in some areas because of the traffic. I had to attend to coverage duties involving the historic visit of Soviet leader Mikhail Gorbachev to Beijing in mid-May. So, I dropped my relatives off at Tiananmen Square to walk around among the students while I went to go park across the street from the Great Hall of the People. They enjoyed mixing around with the demonstrators. Some students spoke English to them. Protestors took off their homemade, sweat-stained headbands and gave them to my uncle and cousin. Chinese characters in black and red ink were written across the headbands, which my relatives took back to the States as souvenirs.

A man looks at refrigerators in a Shanghai store. China's open economic policy brought greater personal prosperity and new ideas to many Chinese. Student protests at Tiananmen expanded to seek democracy in the government. Photo by Noël-Marie Fletcher.

The situation at the square began to deteriorate. My uncle became anxious to leave. I booked their flights out from Beijing to Shanghai and onto the States. It was mid-May at that time.

My maid in the apartment scoffed at first about the student demonstrators. But as days passed, she and other Chinese spectators had an attitude change. Chinese people naturally are extremely found of children and the younger generation. In modern Chinese history, student protestors also played a heroic role in standing up against excesses in society, which helped usher in the Communist movement in China.

A young People's Liberation Army soldier looks at electronics in a store. As the protests continued, it was said the PLA general in charge of Beijing refused to fire on the students at Tiananmen Square. So soldiers from the south were used to massacre those in the square at night. Photo by Noël-Marie Fletcher.

During the Tiananmen movement, student protestors were joined by ordinary people. From my apartment window, I watched a major protest in which carload after carload of ordinary factory workers waved in jubilation from open-back trucks as they drove to Tiananmen Square to join the movement.

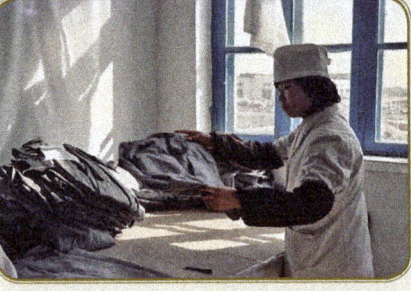

A boy (above), who appears to be a child laborer, at a textile factory in China. A young woman stacks shirts for export at a factory in Dalian. The student protest at Tiananmen Square expanded as ordinary factory workers joined the students. I witnessed great euphoria among the people. Businesses stopped working as the protests continued unabated each day. Photos by Noël-Marie Fletcher.

My apartment had a birds-eye view of a major street leading to the square, which was in close proximity. My work became more difficult. Ordinary people working at companies and in offices stopped going to their jobs. No one picked up the phone when I tried calling places for interviews. Goods stopped flowing into Beijing. Foreign companies became jittery about the safety of their expatriates and their families. Everyone kept waiting for the central government to drop the hammer.

Illness broke out at the square. Pink eye and other maladies. Ambulances began to scream back and forth at all hours in front of my apartment. Sleep became difficult. The government decided to switch off the hot water at about that time. It seemed as if the annual energy conservation shutoff came earlier than normal. I had to boil multiple kettles of water just to take a bath.

A view of Beijing from my bedroom window. On the street below was an artery to Tiananmen Square. It was busy with protestors, ambulances and later military tanks. Photo by Noël-Marie Fletcher.

I knew of some Japanese photographers who were manning the square for a news outfit that wanted 24-hour coverage. Fast-food was not widely available in Beijing back then. I felt sorry for these journalists who had nothing to eat or drink in that hot sun. I decided to take it upon myself to provide food for them. Each day, I'd boil eggs, make sandwiches and send drinks to them with a journalist who went there to start a shift.

I also made time to help a radio foreign correspondent friend who had been single-handedly providing coverage at a grueling pace without any help for weeks. Although I wrote for a newspaper, I had early training in broadcast journalism. No one else in our set of friends knew how to write radio news. Since I'd done it before at a couple of radio stations and also wrote TV news broadcasts, I volunteered to lend a hand. I wrote the copy while he aired it.

One night after we finished, we decided to go to Tiananmen Square. That was the night martial law was declared. We wanted to have a look to see what was going on and assess the mood of the crowd. What a mistake! I did not expect the students would assume we were secret police. There had been reports of secret police and sightings of non-students in the square taking pictures of the demonstrators.

Midnight had passed as we boarded his compact car. I jumped into the passenger seat. We were tired, but our adrenaline flowed. We were still pumped up from putting a news broadcast together and drove with anticipation to the square. His car had the 01 journalist designation on the front and back license plates.

The crowd was tense as we drove through. Our car was quickly surrounded. We couldn't move forward or backward. We were at a standstill. Faces, pressed to the glass, peered at us. Some people started hitting the car and rocking it violently as if to overturn it. It was very scary being trapped helplessly inside as people rocked the car. I thought it was obvious that we were foreigners. But a group mentality in a crowd can be very dangerous. We didn't want to get out of the car. A few minutes seemed like hours. Eventually one of the students realized we weren't Chinese authorities and yelled out. The people thinned out around the car, which allowed us to leave.

A journalist license plate on a car belonging to a foreign news organization in Beijing. Photo by Noël-Marie Fletcher.

We drove off as quickly as possible, trying to avoid hitting people. Beijing residents had more contact with foreigners since they lived in a capital city. However, many demonstrators filling the square were from all over China, which meant some of them were totally unfamiliar with foreigners and foreign journalists.

In late May, I learned that U.S. businessmen were evacuating from Beijing. I broke the story about it. Days later, other reporters and U.S. TV networks were trying to chase the story for information.

Without taxis and companies open, it was very difficult for me to get around in the city. Sometimes I drove and other times I had to walk long distances. After the U.S. companies pulled their people out, I heard that Chinese officials went into the empty offices and began going through files to copy proprietary information. There was lots of speculation among journalists about how long the government would let the situation go on. Most people suspected a violent reaction would end the situation at Tiananmen Square. No one knew when or how.

A train station in central China. Chinese traveled from all over the country to join the protests in Beijing. Photo by Noël-Marie Fletcher.

Civilization had begun to unravel before my eyes in the city. Students made bold demands on the government. No one thought the government would remain silent forever. Many news organizations and reporters were weary of the situation, which had lasted for over a month. It was hard to stay on constant alert for such a long period of time.

I left Beijing after June 1 to start law school in Los Angeles. I had been accepted and planned to begin in the summer program. I attended my first day of class and returned to my temporary lodging. My mind constantly wondered about events in Beijing, where I had left my beloved dog Paloma with a family member there.

The next morning, I awoke to news breaking about the Tiananmen massacre. I called the law school, telling the people there I was returning to Beijing and instructing them to process my disenrollment. They were upset since the program had barely begun. They refused to provide a refund. I didn't care. I jumped into my rental car, dropped it off in the parking lot at the Los Angeles International Airport with the keys in a rental car box, and ran into the terminal. No one at the airport knew what to do. Lots of flights were cancelled. Airline personnel tried to discourage me from traveling to Beijing. I wouldn't listen. I was determined to help my family member and rescue my dog.

I caught the first flight into Beijing from Los Angeles via San Francisco. I phoned my family member in Beijing with information about my arrival and made arrangements to be picked up at the airport. On the airplane, I was among about 20 mostly overseas Chinese passengers. The whole plane was practically empty. Everyone onboard was nervous—from the stewardesses to the passengers. We left our seats to gather together in the middle section to talk. Some passengers stood and some sat. Fear reigned. We didn't know what we would find or if our plane would even be able to land. Information about the Tiananmen massacre was still coming in as our plane left U.S. soil. At that time, the airplanes had smoking sections. I nervously smoked

I decided to go to law school in January 1989. Above is a letter of recommendation that my editor Phil wrote for me to use in my law school applications. I gained admission to a law school in Los Angeles. I attended for one day in June 1989 and left the following day to fly back to Beijing upon hearing about the Tiananmen massacre.

A jeep factory in China. After foreign businessmen left China due to the instability, I heard that Chinese officials raided unattended offices to obtain company records and documents since the foreign businessmen weren't there. Photos by Noël-Marie Fletcher.

lots of cigarettes all the way there.

I arrived at the Beijing airport the night after the Tiananmen massacre. The airport was deserted. My family member picked me up and drove me to a hotel next to the airport. There were lots of troops with guns all along the road to the airport, which was a distance from central Beijing. It was too dangerous to drive back into the city so we stayed at the hotel until daybreak.

That night I learned what happened. I was told that the lights had been turned off at the square. No one could see anything. Tanks and troops had pushed across the upper western portion of the square, killing unsuspecting people in their path by shooting them and running them over. I heard one reporter had been in his hotel on the main road where the military first burst through. Apparently, he heard the commotion and hurriedly phoned his news organization. Then he went to the ground floor where he saw wounded people being brought in bleeding and placed on the lobby floor.

Different journalists were in various locations around the square. After it became clear that the military was killing people, many reporters went to hospitals. I was told that in the darkened hospitals, doctors tried to attend to patients and perform operations using flashlights. There were no official statistics released about the numbers of people killed and injured. I suspect it was well into the thousands. When I had left Beijing earlier, I had seen people taking their small children to the square with them. They behaved as if it was summer fun in the park at night. I kept thinking it was likely that old people and little children were among the victims of the massacre since I'd seen them at the square enjoying themselves with their families.

I heard upon my return to Beijing that the Chinese general in charge of the Beijing area refused to turn his guns on the students and people at the square. For this reason, the central government brought in troops to do the shooting from the Vietnam border—bringing in Chinese soldiers of a different ethnicity, who did not speak the same dialect of Mandarin as people in Beijing.

After spending the night in the hotel, I left the next morning to go to my apartment, where Paloma had been

---

NewsSide — The Journal of Commerce — June 26, 1989

Salute to Noel Fletcher

From Phil Bangsberg, sent May 25, on Noel Fletcher's Beijing work:

I'd like to nominate Noel for at least a Mention in Dispatches.

She's been working very competently and levelheadedly in extremely trying conditions (which is, I know, what all journos are supposed to do, but she's been called upon actually to do it). Communications have been disrupted, food difficult to restock, transport minimal (meaning long walks across a sprawling as well as seething city).

The students have been non-stop processing and driving outside her apartment since the outset, making sleep impossible and travel nearly so.

Getting to contacts was even more difficult than usual, and getting anyone to talk sense a real trial.

Ploughing through the mass of humanity would be daunting for anyone; it was more so for a young, foreign woman, in a country xenophobic even in good times.

Noel's reporting was well ahead of the pack on several occasions: She was first with U.S. companies moving people out, and two days later the U.S. nets and others were still chasing it.

In her spare time, she also found time to help Voice of America's beleaguered correspondent Al Pessin, who was on his own and updating broadcasts hourly for several days without rest.

I think Noel could use some recognition.

(Editor's Note: Ms. Fletcher's courageous and professional coverage resulted in a sizeable bonus from The JofC, in addition to the admiration of all of us here.)

My breaking news coverage and abilities as a reporter during the Tiananmen movement were nominated for special mention by my Hong Kong editor Phil in my newspaper's internal newsletter. The newspaper awarded me with a large bonus for my work.

left alone. The town was nearly empty. I heard there were military snipers located near my apartment building and there had been some type of firefight near there. Vehicles had been upturned and burned.

A Beijing hotel. I had to stay at a hotel near Beijing's airport when I arrived the night after the Tiananmen massacre because it was too dangerous to travel due to a heavy military presence with tanks and armed soldiers throughout the city. Photo by Noël-Marie Fletcher.

Paloma was locked inside. I had to get to her. I went to the building. There was no electricity working, which meant no elevator. The surly maintenance workers on the ground floor were gone. The building was silent. I don't think anyone was in there at all. I climbed the stairs. Paloma was happy to see me. I gathered up her things, some vitamins, liquor, clothing, and food. I couldn't stay in the apartment very long because it was too close to Tiananmen Square to be safe. Military convoys and tanks drove up and down the streets.

I decided that I would stay with other journalists at a friend's apartment, which was located in a diplomatic compound farther away. My friend and his wife opened up their home to as many journalists who could sleep there because it was safer. A bunch of us brought what we had at home to pool our resources. We didn't know how long we'd end up staying there. It was like a fun sleepover. Lots of liquor, caviar from the Soviet Union, vitamins, and not much food. Paloma and I got a bedroom while others slept on the floor.

We'd go out during the day for reporting and return at night after filing our news reports. Lots of military convoys drove around town. We saw soldiers carrying rifles. Helicopters flew overhead constantly. Tanks also were on the streets. When I drove a car down the same roads I'd always traveled before, my car's tires made a new sound driving over asphalt that had been torn by the tread of tanks. The tanks ripped up the streets all over Beijing. We learned to recognize the sound of tanks coming down the street. Everyone was on edge. Some journalists who had gone years without smoking reached for cigarette packs. Lots of us had trouble sleeping.

Some news organizations forced the wives of journalists to leave since they couldn't vouch for their safety. Foreigners started leaving China in droves. I wanted to stay as long as I could to do my job. I contacted the U.S. Embassy to find out if they could help me get Paloma out. The staff was rude. However, I managed to talk to the Ambassador's wife. She had a sympathetic ear since she had a dog, too. She tried to make arrangements for Paloma, but was unable to at the last minute because I wasn't an American diplomat. So much for helping American citizens, I thought.

I contacted my friend with the golden retriever. We heard that a German airline would allow dogs to fly unattended. We went to the hotel where the airline had an office. It was mayhem. Hotel pillars around the lobby had long strips of paper—like streamers—dangling with information for people from their governments. Directions on how to get out of Beijing. We were looking for flights anywhere out of Beijing. My friend was able to get her dog on a flight to Europe and have people pick up the dog in another country. I didn't have anyone who could do that for Paloma. We tried to go to another hotel to look for an airline for me.

Hardly any cars were on the road. Foreigners had created paper signs with the flags of their countries pasted to the windows to ensure they wouldn't be shot at.

We turned one corner and proceeded down a narrow street. A car with Japanese flag signs in the windows drove quickly past us in the opposite direction. The Japanese men in the car were waving their hands frantically at us. We didn't know what was going on. We continued driving forward slowly only to come face-to-face with a tank pointed right at us. We spun the car around and fled as fast as we could.

The situation at the other hotels was the same. Chaos.

Everyone was trying to get out. The stores could not stock food. The grocery store opened for foreigners would only sell people

Young men walk along the street in the summer. Buses like the one in the back were upturned in various places in Beijing as people tried to create roadblocks to stop the military. Photo by Noël-Marie Fletcher.

food if they lived in the diplomatic compound next door. If you lived at another compound, you were out of luck. All hotel restaurants—a mainstay for foreigners—had closed except for one that served a buffet with canned food.

With no mail service or newspapers, it was difficult for most people to get information. Taxis stopped running. No vehicles were entering or leaving the city. Some Chinese people had turned over trucks over to try to create roadblocks to stop military troops. No one could get gas to refill vehicles. Not even journalists. All people had for their cars was what was already inside their gas tanks.

Food was flying off shelves. A Canadian journalist friend got into a fistfight with someone over a loaf of bread. I saw an American diplomat I knew who worked with reporters. He had plastic bags weighing down his arms with food that he'd just bought from the Friendship Store where I was heading. I was so angry. He could shop at the American store run by the U.S. Embassy. Why was he hoarding food from one of the last few places where ordinary people could get food from?

There were even fewer Chinese people at work anywhere. Expressing fears about the future in China, normally bad-tempered Chinese elevator operators urged foreigners to leave the country.

Hundreds of people along the main streets by some of the main diplomatic compounds sat on the roofs of buildings to watch troops and tanks drive past. I couldn't believe it. They looked so relaxed, squatting on rooftops or sitting with their legs dangling below. It was almost like they were passing the time at some kind of recreational event.

Some of the windows of the areas where foreigners lived had their windows shot up by patrolling troops. Tanks had been stationed on the streets for days.

A PLA soldier takes a photo of a child in a park in Beijing. After the Tiananmen massacre, there were PLA soldiers throughout the city in trucks, along streets, and in tanks in Beijing. Photo by Noël-Marie Fletcher.

A hotel in China. Hotels were central locations for businesses and food for those living in Beijing. Many companies had offices and their employees based in hotels. Photo by Noël-Marie Fletcher.

Still working on the problem of Paloma, I heard that the U.S. Embassy had made plans to operate from one place instead of their three locations. A few men had volunteered to stay behind if need be and were following a directive to shred documents.

At night, the sound of gunfire could be heard. The situation was volatile. I learned the only way to get Paloma out of Beijing was to fly out with her myself. So I made arrangements to leave Beijing.

On June 8, I took a taxi to the airport with my dog. The cab driver charged me $100 in U.S. currency since he could name his price during the crisis. We made the long trip past many military convoys with heavily armed troops. When I got to the airport, I didn't know it, but I had a seat on the last U.S. flight evacuated out of Beijing. I felt lucky. I did not have to pay for the flight since it was an evacuation. I only had to show my passport. The State Department billed me three months later. I arrived early in the morning and sat on the floor with my dog in the lobby. A nice old Chinese airline worker took my luggage. He rummaged around and found a cucumber to give Paloma. She happily chewed it all up. I didn't think she'd eat it, but she did with glee. While checking in with the airlines, I heard that U.S. diplomats received a call alerting them to military troops looting two buildings in Beijing where most foreign companies had their offices.

Views of two hotels in China. After the Tiananmen massacre, hotels in Beijing had instructions posted about evacuations for different countries. Also hotels began to run out of food. Photos by Noël-Marie Fletcher.

Inside the airport, people of all nationalities were sitting all over the floors, chairs and anywhere else they could. It was like the Tower of Babel with so many languages being spoken. I recall thinking it looked like the United Nations in that airport that day. I attracted a lot of attention sitting there with my pretty dog. Nearby was my Pakistani neighbor, a diplomat, trying to console his crying three-year-old daughter. An American businessman comforted his young Chinese bride. Paloma and I sat on the floor for hours. A group of young Irish children parked themselves next to Paloma for several hours and entertained themselves by feeding her crackers. Everyone had their belongings scattered around.

We all shared stories about having to leave at a moment's notice. Most people were only allowed to bring two suitcases per person. In my suitcase, I packed personal photos, financial records, my astrakhan fur coat, a small Indian rug, a crocodile purse that I bought in Thailand, a cobra belt, a jade statue of a Chinese peasant girl holding up a lantern, a ceramic button of Chairman Mao from the Cultural Revolution, and Mao's Little Red Book of Communist Party doctrines. With no electricity in my apartment, I had to climb 11 flights of stairs, throw things into two suitcases, and make it back down the stairs holding both heavy suitcases.

We kept hearing at different times that our flight would leave. We'd prepare to get ready. Then we got news that the government closed the airport. There were Chinese military officers and soldiers everywhere staring coldly at everyone. It was nerve-racking. I remember watching a local TV channel turned on inside the terminal. It had a show of knitting with close-ups of a woman's hands moving knitting needles in and out of a small patch of woolen cloth. The show played over again all day long.

Even though I had arrived early in the morning, I didn't board my flight until 11:30 p.m. There was no food. My poor dog was so good. I had her with me until I boarded the plane when a worker came for her. I flew on an American airline carrier since it was a U.S. government evacuation. The other passengers and I had to walk single file past Chinese military officers just as we were about to board the plane. I saw a few people suddenly get snatched from the line ahead of me by the military and escorted away. I don't know who they were, but they didn't catch that flight.

A photo of me and Paloma at the airport awaiting our evacuation from Beijing appeared in newspapers all over the United States.

Once aboard the plane, I was among 68 people. Everyone was so happy. The pilot greeted us, telling us he how glad he was to be taking us away to Tokyo. You could tell he was American by the way he spoke. He was joking. Everyone onboard cheered loudly and clapped their hands. I told the stewardess I needed a drink. Other people wanted a dose of alcohol as well. But since the flight was a U.S. government evacuation, there would be no alcohol. We were all so upset. It had been a harrowing experience. We didn't know until the last minute whether we could even leave Beijing.

The plane took us to Narita Airport in Japan, which had been designated as the nearest airport from Beijing to the States. From there we would have to make our own way home or to whatever destination we wanted. The Japanese were fabulous. The airport was supposed to be closed due to noise restrictions. Our flight had been so delayed that we arrived hours after it closed, but the Japanese government ordered the whole airport to open just for our plane.

We were treated like royalty with warm welcomes. The Japanese had set up tables to assist groups of passengers as we stepped off the plane. When I asked about Paloma, I was told they brought in a special animal quarantine officer to personally ensure she was well cared for. I found out later they even fed her steak after her arrival on Japanese soil. Airport personnel set up special phone banks for us to call for free our relatives anywhere in the world to let them know we were okay. Next they had arranged for a new hotel, which had not yet been opened to the public, to provide accommodations for us. We paid for nothing. Everything was provided freely. Like everyone else, I had a special person assigned to help me

Paloma and I appeared in newspapers in the United States and overseas in a photo taken as we awaited a U.S. government evacuation flight out of Beijing.

arrange a flight to my destination the next day. I was told to sleep in as long as I wanted and then call.

At breakfast the following morning, I spoke with other Americans who had been on the flight with me to exchange stories. Many had been living in different cities in China. One group of American women left over 100 American men behind at a coal mine in Shanxi Province where they worked. The women told me they had passed around Valium like candy to each other to calm their nerves during the evacuation ordeal. Other Americans described huddling around shortwave radios listening to American and British news reports when they heard about the Tiananmen massacre. I heard stories of Chinese officials trying to stop Americans from leaving the country. The Chinese partners in one joint venture accused the Americans of breaking their contract when they tried to leave. The Americans were prevented from leaving because the Chinese refused to provide interpreters or transportation to the airport. When the Americans and their wives hired a taxi convoy, they were locked out of the airport and told their airplane would not leave. The group was only allowed to board the flight after their top American boss in Beijing called the local Chinese mayor.

In Tokyo, I heard from a U.S. diplomat about the Chinese government stopping airplanes from flying into China to evacuate foreign nationals. He told me about a chartered U.S. airplane that was held for 48 hours. It was refused landing rights after arriving in Shanghai from Japan. On the next try, it got as far as Shanghai and then traveled further to Beijing, where it was not allowed to land. On its third flight to China, it had the okay to land in Beijing, which it did, but then no people were allowed onto the flight since the airplane lacked permission to board passengers. This anecdote helped explain the hurdles that must have been involved in getting my flight out of Beijing as I waited at the airport for more than 12 hours during the evacuation.

When it was time for me to go to the airport, I met a wonderful Japanese woman who came to my hotel. She escorted me to the airport, made my flight arrangements to San Francisco, Los Angeles and New Mexico, and even took me to see my dog Paloma before I caught my flight out of Tokyo.

After being in transit for more than 24 hours, Paloma and I arrived in Albuquerque where my relatives were. A local TV station heard I was arriving, but missed me at the airport. I was interviewed a few days later by a TV network in New York City.

I phoned my editors at the *Journal of Commerce* and dictated a story over the telephone about my experiences in the evacuation. I had taken notes and interviewed people during the ordeal in a continuation of my journalist work.

I remained in the States for two weeks of rest before flying back to Beijing one last time—without Paloma. I wanted her to remain safe with family because I didn't know what life in Beijing would be like upon my return.

The Journal of Co
and Commercial
TUESDAY, JUNE 13, 1989

Evacuee Voices Fear for Future

By NOEL FLETCHER
Journal of Commerce Special

Correspondent Fletcher has spent the past three years covering Hong Kong and China for The Journal of Commerce. Here is her own account of her departure from strife-torn Beijing:

Even though I'm safe in the United States after being evacuated from China late last week, I can't stop worrying about what I left behind.

What will be the fate of my Chinese and American friends? Will my apartment, hastily abandoned like so many others, be looted? How will China regain the economic success and prosperity lost in less than three months after 10 solid years of hard work?

A few hours before I boarded

SEE **EVACUEE**, PAGE 3A

The front page of my newspaper, The Journal of Commerce, with my article that I dictated over the phone to my editor in New York City after I arrived safely in the United States from Beijing.

Part 4: Final Months in China

Chapter 10: Post-Tiananmen Crackdown

Beijing was like a ghost town when I returned two weeks after being evacuated. Walking and driving around the city was like being in a Wild West movie—you're outside on deserted streets, feeling a million eyes on you while everyone appears to be gone except for a few people hiding and peeking out from behind curtains. Everywhere I drove, the steering wheel on the car vibrated as the car tires drove over the rough grooves that the tanks clawed into the street pavement. I had to try to maneuver the car away from those ruts, which could cause the steering wheel to jerk aside suddenly.

Life as I knew it before the protests had disappeared. Everywhere I went near Tiananmen Square, including the main roads near it, bore evidence of violence: mostly clusters of bullet holes and shattered windowpanes.

It was difficult to go to one of my favorite Asian restaurants alongside the southern section of the square. All around the front door, the exterior of the building looked like it'd had a bad case of acne due to pitting—but the small round holes were from bullets. I wasn't alone among my journalist friends in thinking it likely that people died there. We just didn't know who or how many perished. I felt like the place was haunted. I tried to avoid going there. I wasn't able to partake in the good food, fun conversation and general merriment as I had done before the Tiananmen Square massacre.

Along one of the main streets was one diplomatic apartment up several floors that I used to see while driving past. It was said to be the home of U.S. Embassy head of security—the guy who had dressed up as Dracula for the American Halloween party. I

A PLA officer on a billboard in Beijing. There were few foreigners left in China in the months following the Tiananmen massacre, and even fewer foreign women. Photo by Noël-Marie Fletcher.

heard that the Americans were having an emergency all-hands meeting at one of their offices to discuss the deteriorating condition of China after the Tiananmen Square massacre. While everyone was away, only the man's two children remained at home with their Chinese maid. At that time, the Chinese military fired armor-piercing bullets into this man's apartment. I heard the Chinese maid threw herself on top of the two children to shield them as bullets flew through the apartment. I was told the bullets also penetrated not only the walls but passed through books and other items in the apartment. I was told that it was after this incident that the U.S. Embassy decided to evacuate everyone except that small group of volunteer paper shredders. I heard that if the Chinese had really wanted to kill the people in the apartment they would have done so; the firing on this apartment was rather a warning to the U.S. diplomatic corps in Beijing.

Hardly any foreign women remained in Beijing after the Tiananmen massacre except for those too poor to have been evacuated—the ones from the Middle East and Africa. All dependents (women and kids) within the expatriate community were gone. It wasn't safe for them to return. The wives of

My Time in Another World

A few Chinese people walk next to barriers at Tiananmen Square. After the massacre, Chinese people avoided going to the square, which was under heavy government surveillance. Photo by Noël-Marie Fletcher.

my journalist friends left. The wives of the businessmen I knew were gone, too. I numbered among only a handful of American women journalists in the foreign press corps. This dynamic also was strange—adding to the surreal world I felt I now lived in.

The Chinese government began a public campaign immediately after my return to Beijing in which they blamed foreign intervention, particularly from U.S. agents, for the protests. Chinese newspapers carried articles slamming the West. The Chinese government slid notes under the doors threatening foreign journalists. I received one under the door of my apartment. It was written in Chinese and English with threats about news coverage. The note ordered journalists to carry their passports at all times for identification.

Myself and other journalists I knew were very angry at the government for what it had done and for its increasing harassment of us. The guards at my diplomatic compound had become aggressive since the massacre. They acted confrontational during my comings and goings.

One day I walked to the Friendship Store to buy some groceries. I had a heavy plastic bag weighing each of my wrists down as I walked slowly to the entrance of my apartment compound. One young tough in a military uniform leveled his semi-automatic rifle at me. I was less than a car length away from him when he did this. I became enraged. Clearly I lived there and was returning home with my shopping. I was no threat at all. I couldn't even lift my arms since I toted two heavy plastic bags. I started yelling at him in English and Mandarin. I didn't care if he shot me. I dared him to. I got right in his face. He took a few steps back, lowering his rifle. I shut up and continued walking across the parking lot. If he was trying to frighten me, it didn't work. I should have been scared, but I wasn't. That notion of being afraid didn't even occur to me. Instead my outraged thoughts went along the lines of, "How dare you!"

A PLA soldier looks at a poster for American cigarettes. Photo by Noël-Marie Fletcher.

The Chinese government began installing small cameras, like the ones you see nowadays at street intersections, all over the city. Some of these cameras had little windshield wipers on them. Many of these cameras were turned on building doorways instead of at roadway intersections. I remember looking at the entrance to one popular hotel for foreign journalists and expatriates. It must have had at least half dozen cameras installed in various positions to monitor different angles of the front door and parking lot.

What bothered me the most was that ordinary Chinese people stopped talking to me since I was a foreigner. I didn't blame them. It was hard though. I was walking in a park one day and saw a little child playing. I thought the child was cute and went over to say hello. The parents rushed over and pulled the kid away from me like I was a monster.

Another time I attended a Catholic Mass one Sunday. I sat in a pew like I did from time to time. People were scattered here and there, like they usually were. I was lost in thought for about 10 minutes. Then I looked around and noticed all the people had moved away from me, in silence, apparently one by one. There was nobody near me at all. I felt like I had the plague. It happened in restaurants, too. If I tried to make a joke or say anything at all when a Chinese person brought me my food or the bill, they would stare and say as little as possible. Afterwards, they left quickly.

Recreational areas in China. After the military crackdown following the Tiananmen Square massacre, I had difficulty trying to interact with ordinary Chinese people. They avoided me and even pulled their children away if I approached because they were fearful about government reprisals. Photos by Noël-Marie Fletcher.

All the normal and nice interactions I had with people were at an end. I was a risk to their safety. This avoidance of me made it easier for to leave China a few months later. It was already an isolating place, but when people didn't even want to talk to me it was even worse.

I didn't have much to do in my spare time so I started going to antique markets that once had been frequented by the wives of Beijing diplomats. The sellers at the markets were frantic to earn money. The diplomat wives were all gone. They had almost no customers. I spent a lot of time there wandering around. I made select purchases of furniture and decorative items. I wanted to know about the symbolism on the carvings, the types of wood used, etc. I enjoyed learning new things from my conversations there. That was practically the only time ordinary Chinese people talked to me like a normal person instead of avoiding me.

Many times after the massacre, I saw military jeeps patrolling the streets. I also witnessed Chinese people being grabbed off the streets by soldiers from military jeeps. The way it worked was that a jeep drove up suddenly to an unsuspecting person walking on foot or riding a bike. The jeep stopped in front of the person and soldiers sprang out, grabbing the person. Once I had just finished eating at a hotel restaurant. I started driving away when I saw this. I pulled over the car immediately along the side of the road and ran across the street just in time to see the soldiers throw a coat over the person, who was shoved into the jeep. As I arrived at the scene, clouds of dust swirled in the air as the jeep sped away. Several ordinary Chinese people, on foot and on bicycles, had stopped to watch. I tried to ask them in Mandarin about what happened. Although they didn't talk to me directly, they provided me with answers in a very clever way. They spoke to each other very loud, repeating sentences a few times to ensure I understood. It was something along the lines like: "Did you see them take away that man?" "Yes, he was walking along the street." "He was alone." While they didn't answer me directly, I could tell they were deliberately conveying answers to me by their exaggerated dialogue with each other.

The government crackdown was in full swing. I had heard a Chinese saying that if you kill one person, you warn 100. This was the aftermath I witnessed following the Tiananmen massacre. The government rhetoric was intense to discredit the uprising. Even before this, the government could be untruthful and maintained stances to meet its own goals that seemed unbelievable at times.

A case in point was the government's stance on Taiwan—a separate country, which they refused to acknowledge as a separate country. I had heard they had a name-only government representative for Taiwan who wasn't from Taiwan. When I interviewed Chinese officials, I had to be careful if they were discussing Hainan Island near the Vietnam border. They'd describe Hainan as being China's second-largest island (after Taiwan!). In reality, Hainan was China's largest island. I remember watching the weather on TV news in Beijing. I'd shake my head and laugh to myself when the show included the temperatures of Taiwan each day in the weather newscast.

With the Tiananmen uprising and massacre, the central government decided to hold an exhibit at a military museum in Beijing for all to see about the foreign intervention. I went to this with some journalist friends. There we saw items taken from the protests. I posed for a photo in front of a Chinese tank. Many pictures were on display showing various scenes from

Just before the Tiananmen Square movement started, I had a craving for an American chocolate candy bar. So I drove to an American hotel gift shop to buy the candy and picked up an International Herald Tribune newspaper. That day I was very moved when I read the obituary of Empress Zita, the last Empress of Austria-Hungary. She lived a heroic life after the premature death of her husband Emperor Karl, the last emperor of the Habsburg Dynasty. I was impressed that she and her eldest son Otto had bravely resisted Hitler, who chased her through Europe until she fled to safety with her family during World War II. I became determined that if I ever had a daughter, she would be named Zita after Empress Zita. After I left Beijing, I indeed had a daughter, and I named her Zita.

The view out the dining room of my Beijing apartment. Photo by Noël-Marie Fletcher.

the protests. The photos were blown up to huge sizes for people to take a good look at. "Finally," I thought, "here is the evidence of the secret police taking those photos I heard about at the square."

My friends and I laughed when we saw a photo showing an American journalist with a distorted expression at the square. My Chinese Casanova acquaintance named Lyle started to freak out. He thought his photo might have been taken since he went to the square all the time to socialize with friends and interpret. He went into hiding and rode in trains from one city to another to avoid capture. Since he did a lot of work for American journalists, multiple efforts were made on his behalf to help him leave China for his safety. He pulled these strings and those from his well-connected Communist parents to get a ticket out of Beijing to the U.S.A. before the Chinese military captured him.

Myself and my journalist friends heard about students being arrested throughout Beijing. We heard rumors about hundreds of students being imprisoned in different universities in the city. As I said, we were angry at the government. We wanted to find out anything we could about the massacre and students because the government was minimizing the entire incident.

We decided to take turns on different nights driving past roadblocks to various quadrants of the city to look for imprisoned students. In hindsight, this was not a smart move—as I found out. After we filed our articles with our news editors outside China, we'd sit in newsrooms to complain about the situation. After some cigarettes and a couple of shots of liquor, some of us would go patrolling. Everyone wondered if anyone would do anything at the end of the 100-day Chinese mourning period.

One night, about 100 days after the massacre, I took my last trip doing this. I'm a good driver and know how to handle a car at high speeds and in tight maneuvers better than most men. Also I enjoyed the element of surprise I had as a woman driver whenever I was stopped by Chinese soldiers.

At around midnight, I drove out of the wire service office. I slowed as I came to a checkpoint with about 40 military convoy trucks parked along both sides of a street. All traffic was stopped and identities checked. When I drove to the head of the line, I watched in amusement as the officers looked from my ID to my face and back again in disbelief. A few seconds later, they waved me through. I never had to say a word. I continued driving for 30 minutes through the deserted city. A curfew had been imposed. I turned down a circular road leaving a highway on my way to a university area.

Newspapers in my apartment in Beijing. I read lots of newspapers to keep busy and keep informed about life outside of China. Photo by Noël-Marie Fletcher.

As I turned the steering wheel slowly while exiting the highway, a young soldier with an automatic rifle jumped out of the bushes next to the road to ambush me. He had been hidden in the darkness. He seemed as scared of my car's sudden appearance as much as I was frightened of him when he jumped out pointing the rifle.

I slowed to a stop but was prepared to floor the gas in case I needed to flee. I hesitated again and then came to a stop. He raised his rifle to shoot. He was shaking and screaming, pointing his rifle at me outside my window. I rolled down my window and handed him my passport. He was speaking in Chinese but I didn't understand what he was saying. I tried speaking to him many times in Mandarin. He did not understand me. He screamed again and threw my passport in my face.

With his rifle pointed at me and his finger near the trigger, he motioned to me to get out of the car. I didn't know what to do. Then I remembered having heard that the Chinese soldiers who fired on the students were of a different ethnic group from the Vietnam border and unable to speak Mandarin. That would explain why he didn't understand me, especially since I spoke with a Beijing accent. Clearly he didn't read English since he threw my passport at me, nearly hitting me in the face with it. The soldier steadily became more agitated, screaming louder and motioning at me with his rifle. I remembered that I had my Chinese driver's license with me. It would tell him I was an American journalist. I reached into my purse and handed it to him. He backed away from the car, lowered his rifle, and examined the driver's license. It seemed to satisfy him. He calmed down a bit.

Still yelling at me, he motioned for me to leave. I put my license back in my purse. I was shaking like a leaf. I knew what a close call I'd had. A very close call. I was so shaken that I didn't want to proceed any further. Instead I drove back to the diplomatic compound. When I got home at the end of the outing, I must have smoked a whole pack of cigarettes to settle my nerves and I had a couple of shots of booze. No more busting through roadblocks after the nightly curfew for me.

The last major event I covered in Beijing before leaving was the 40th Anniversary of the founding of the People's Republic of China. On Oct. 1, 1989, a grand celebration was held at Tiananmen Square. The nation's leaders stood on a rostrum near the entrance to the Forbidden City. Security was tight. Cars had to park a distance from the festivities. The central government had been gearing up for this event with great fanfare. All types of commemorative pins, paper fans and other items were being distributed. I took several as souvenirs.

I attended this event with some journalists. A crowd of VIPs and members of the diplomatic corps occupied places of honor. The finale was a tremendous firework display. I loved Chinese fireworks, particularly those displayed for New Year's Eve and Chinese New Year in Hong Kong. I'd never before seen so many spectacular colors, patterns and variations. Those all paled in comparison to the ones lit off in Beijing that Sunday night. Booming sounds filled the air. A thick scent of gunpowder filled my nostrils. Glistening firework displays sparkled, exploded and re-exploded nonstop for the longest time. It was breathtaking. It felt like being inside the beating heart of that pulsating, exotic nation.

During one of my many visits to the Forbidden City.

When I walked to the car after the celebration, my ears rang from the din—similar to what I'd experienced when leaving loud rock concerts. The exterior of the car was covered with thick black soot from the gunpowder debris that rained down after the firework explosions.

That night, people seemed nonchalant that blood had been spilled only a few months earlier on that very square—which had also been the ancient site of other historic battles and bloodshed. Life went on.

I left Beijing at the end of October 1989. I had grown tired of being a foreigner in Asia. I had considered a move to London but thought it was time to go home to the States. I'd had many dangerous close calls and had nearly been shot.

I wanted to be among my own people in my own country and enjoy the things I liked about the U.S. My furniture was shipped by train to Shanghai and onwards to California.

My last stopover in Asia was in Hong Kong. I bid farewell

I'm standing at the doorway of my Beijing apartment during my final year in China. I'm wearing my favorite Chinese men's shoes.

to my journalist friends in Beijing, boarding my last flight out of China. I arrived at night in Hong Kong. To celebrate, I had arranged for a limo to pick me up at Kai Tak airport and take me to a luxury hotel in Hong Kong. I had lots of luggage since I'd been abroad for a few years. When I checked into the hotel, I started chatting with the Hong Kong Chinese staff. I told them I was a journalist moving from Beijing back to the United States. They were very interested in the situation in China because it was still in flux. I described covering the Tiananmen uprising and aftermath. They wanted me to provide some details about what I had experienced. They listened to every word intently. They were very happy to learn about it from someone who had first-hand knowledge. They were very upset about the violence. It was very touching to talk to them. When I finally got situated in my hotel room with all my luggage, I received the largest fruit basket and loveliest floral arrangement I'd ever seen.

These were gifts sent to me from the hotel management as tokens of appreciation. They were grateful for my public service as a foreign journalist providing news about Tiananmen and the situation in China.

The End

About the Author

Noël-Marie Fletcher is a career print and broadcast journalist who has lived and worked in Asia and Europe.

As a financial journalist, she covered international trade in many Asian countries including Hong Kong, South Korea, Singapore and Thailand.

As a Beijing Correspondent, she was one of the few female journalists living in China who experienced the events surrounding the Tiananmen Square uprising. She has also worked as a journalist in Palm Springs and in broadcast television in the San Francisco Bay area.

She is the author of numerous nonfiction books. She served as Acting Bureau Chief for *The Times* of London in Berlin in 2017. She is a reciprocal member of the National Press Club in Washington, D.C. and a member of the Geneva Press Club.

Books by Noël-Marie Fletcher

Captives of the Southwest

Take a journey into the lives of people who vanished in the Wild West. Explore true stories and eyewitness accounts of the kidnappings and experiences of Anglos, Hispanics, and Native Americans taken captive in New Mexico and the Southwest.

Each chapter takes the reader into a unique setting alongside new casts of characters—including lost settlers, greedy prospectors, elusive desert traders, vigilante lawmen, nomadic tribesmen, courageous women and resilient children. Stunning historical and modern photographs provide vivid glimpses into the life of each captive and the environments they experienced. Includes rich illustrations: 115 historic photos, 14 maps, 35 news articles, 40+ modern photos as well as interesting historical details and rare images of key people and places described.

Includes rich illustrations: 115 historic photos, 14 maps, 35 news articles, 40+ modern photos as well as interesting historical details and rare images of key people and places described. Author and researcher Noël-Marie Fletcher provides a local perspective and expert analysis for events and stories A rare gem for readers of Wild West history containing gripping tales of adventure, hardship, and courage.

River of My Ancestors: The Rio Grande in Pictures

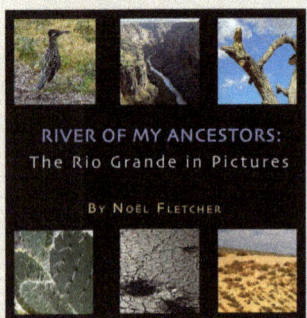

Take a journey along the wild and rugged Rio Grande. Beautiful pictures capture the essence of the famous river and its importance in the arid Southwest. Author/ photographer Noël-Marie Fletcher provides family stories and insights about frontier life with 180 photos.

Pathways in Time: Photo Journeys

Travel along many roads and witness simple and abstract forms of beauty in 160+ photos that show the wonder of nature such as in rainbows, birds, trees, leaves, raindrops, and the earth. It also reveals abstract views of architecture, urban settings, and found objects. Author/photographer Noël-Marie Fletcher shows how to find beauty in ordinary life and the world that surrounds us all.

Windows into the Beauty of Flowers & Nature

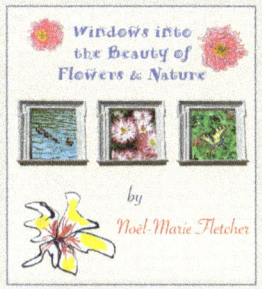

Take a journey into the beauty of life. Featuring over 450 photos that show flowers in their many forms and types in an array of resplendent colors. Stunning high-quality images capture the essences of various insects and animals who live among us, including butterflies, lizards, birds, bees, and rabbits. Author/photographer Noel-Marie Fletcher also compliments her photos by including some of her freehand pastel and ink artwork.

The Strange Side of War by Sarah Macnaughtan & Noël-Marie Fletcher

Accompany Scottish novelist Sarah Macnaughtan as she volunteers alongside British humanitarian groups to alleviate the suffering in war-torn lands. Her many adventures tell unique stories of tragedy and triumph, taking readers on an unforgettable journey from the trenches of Belgium to the distant frontiers of Persia and tsarist Russia. Author/editor Noël-Marie Fletcher provides new historical context that brings Sarah's story to life and helps readers to remember the bravery and sacrifice of those who died. Illustrated with 130+ rare photos and propaganda posters from World War I, this important work features historical insights about the people and places involved in the conflict.

Two Years in the Forbidden City by Princess Der Ling & Noël-Marie Fletcher

This true story was the first eyewitness account of the Imperial Court written by a Chinese aristocrat for Western readers. It provides an up-close view of the notorious Dowager Empress Tzu-hsi in her final years. It includes interesting historical details and photos about China's infamous Dowager Empress, the Boxer Rebellion and the Imperial Court as well as 100+ historical photographs, illustrations, and paintings. Author/editor Noël-Marie Fletcher that provides context for this book in modern Chinese history.

www.ingramcontent.com/pod-product-compliance
Lightning Source LLC
Chambersburg PA
CBHW060836170426
43192CB00019BA/2795